"In *I HRT the Cult Years,* language spills forth in feverish sermons a[nd] incantations and collapse, an attempted song for everyone. This is a[...] belief / an equal unbelief," where we are plagued by digital detritus[, polluting corporations, exploitati]ve politicians, and systemic oppression, and where influencers on Instagram and TikTok peddle balms too good to be true. Relax, attune, focus, and follow Steven Karl on this wild spiritual journey into darkness."

-Gina Myers
author of *Hold it Down*

"Steven Karl's *I HRT the Cult Years* critiques and embodies the cult leader at the center of the book who, in turn, critiques and embodies the American society that bred him. The overflowing and excessive ritual and repetition enacted throughout these poems build out a vision of what Svetlana Boym called "restorative nostalgia" – an alluring and fatal vision."

-Dan Magers
author of *Party Knife*

"The diastolic pause in a pulse, crossed with a moss-covered Mobius strip, Steven Karl's conflicted psalms approach from all directions, borderless, bare, hiding their hiddenness inside the language of direct address. They shout "Hallelujah" from a mystic abyss. This book is a sound-bath of spells and screams. I suggest singing along."

-Eric Baus
author of *How I Became a Hum*

"Steven Karl's book will put you in a trance and deliver you to the edge of insanity. Like the songbook of a fanatic *I HRT the Cult Years* will fascinate and disturb. I could not look away."

-Ben Mirov
author of *ghost machines*

Cover art by Joseph Lappie

ISBN: 978-1-952055-57-7

I HRT THE CULT YEARS:

EMPTY EMPIRE OF AFTERSONG

Steven Karl

Table of Contents

"It ought to be distinctly felt by us that we stand in the midst of two worlds, the world of matter and the world of spirit. Our bodies belong to one..." -Ralph Waldo Emerson

"I had nothing to dream/So I dreamt of you/Has this all come about/Just because of you?" -Swervedriver, "Mary Winter"

"...for nostalgia to operate, we must in fact forget aspects of the actual past and substitute a sentimetal myth about how things might have been, or the objects we never possessed." - Lincoln Geraghty

"No one really knows the way you feel/But all the kids say they adore you/How it bores you, it's so unreal/ It makes you feel so small/'til you don't feel at all/It makes you look for signs, secret signs" -Bettie Serveert, "The Link"

Quietly fell in love I for lie & denial & look at this tree Can you not feel the weight of God shadow
Quietly fell in love I for lie & denial & look at this tree Can you not feel the weight of God shadow
Quietly fell in love I for lie & denial & look at this tree Can you not feel the weight of God shadow
Quietly fell in love I for lie & denial & look at this tree Can you not feel the weight of God shadow
Quietly fell in love I for lie & denial & look at this tree Can you not feel the weight of God shadow
The spirit is in me. I am the spirit. So heavy this country I need not forgiveness. I am the spirit.
The spirit is in me. I am the spirit. So heavy this country I need not forgiveness. I am the spirit.
The spirit is in me. I am the spirit. So heavy this country I need not forgiveness. I am the spirit.
Quietly fell in love I for lie & denial & look at this tree Can you not feel the weight of God shadow
Quietly fell in love I for lie & denial & look at this tree Can you not feel the weight of God shadow
Quietly fell in love I for lie & denial & look at this tree Can you not feel the weight of God shadow
Quietly fell in love I for lie & denial & look at this tree Can you not feel the weight of God shadow
Quietly fell in love I for lie & denial & look at this tree Can you not feel the weight of God shadow
Quietly fell in love I for lie & denial & look at this tree Can you not feel the weight of God shadow
Quietly fell in love I for lie & denial & look at this tree Can you not feel the weight of God shadow
Quietly fell in love I for lie & denial & look at this tree Can you not feel the weight of God shadow
Quietly fell in love I for lie & denial & look at this tree Can you not feel the weight of God shadow
Quietly fell in love I for lie & denial & look at this tree Can you not feel the weight of God shadow
The spirit is in me. I am the spirit. So heavy this country I need not forgiveness. I am the spirit.
The spirit is in me. I am the spirit. So heavy this country I need not forgiveness. I am the spirit.
The spirit is in me. I am the spirit. So heavy this country I need not forgiveness. I am the spirit.
Quietly fell in love I for lie & denial & look at this tree Can you not feel the weight of God shadow
Quietly fell in love I for lie & denial & look at this tree Can you not feel the weight of God shadow
Quietly fell in love I for lie & denial & look at this tree Can you not feel the weight of God shadow
Quietly fell in love I for lie & denial & look at this tree Can you not feel the weight of God shadow
Quietly fell in love I for lie & denial & look at this tree Can you not feel the weight of God shadow
Quietly fell in love I for lie & denial & look at this tree Can you not feel the weight of God shadow
Quietly fell in love I for lie & denial & look at this tree Can you not feel the weight of God shadow
Quietly fell in love I for lie & denial & look at this tree Can you not feel the weight of God shadow
Quietly fell in love I for lie & denial & look at this tree Can you not feel the weight of God shadow
Quietly fell in love I for lie & denial & look at this tree Can you not feel the weight of God shadow

Quietly fell in love I for lie & denial & look at this tree Can you not feel the weight of God shadow
Quietly fell in love I for lie & denial & look at this tree Can you not feel the weight of God shadow
Quietly fell in love I for lie & denial & look at this tree Can you not feel the weight of God shadow
Quietly fell in love I for lie & denial & look at this tree Can you not feel the weight of God shadow
Quietly fell in love I for lie & denial & look at this tree Can you not feel the weight of God shadow
Quietly fell in love I for lie & denial & look at this tree Can you not feel the weight of God shadow
Quietly fell in love I for lie & denial & look at this tree Can you not feel the weight of God shadow
Quietly fell in love I for lie & denial & look at this tree Can you not feel the weight of God shadow
Quietly fell in love I for lie & denial & look at this tree Can you not feel the weight of God shadow

The spirit is in me. I am the spirit. So heavy this country I need not forgiveness. I am the spirit.
The spirit is in me. I am the spirit. So heavy this country I need not forgiveness. I am the spirit.
The spirit is in me. I am the spirit. So heavy this country I need not forgiveness. I am the spirit.
The spirit is in me. I am the spirit. So heavy this country I need not forgiveness. I am the spirit.
The spirit is in me. I am the spirit. So heavy this country I need not forgiveness. I am the spirit.
The spirit is in me. I am the spirit. So heavy this country I need not forgiveness. I am the spirit.
The spirit is in me. I am the spirit. So heavy this country I need not forgiveness. I am the spirit.
The spirit is in me. I am the spirit. So heavy this country I need not forgiveness. I am the spirit.
The spirit is in me. I am the spirit. So heavy this country I need not forgiveness. I am the spirit.
The spirit is in me. I am the spirit. So heavy this country I need not forgiveness. I am the spirit.
The spirit is in me. I am the spirit. So heavy this country I need not forgiveness. I am the spirit.
The spirit is in me. I am the spirit. So heavy this country I need not forgiveness. I am the spirit.
The spirit is in me. I am the spirit. So heavy this country I need not forgiveness. I am the spirit.
The spirit is in me. I am the spirit. So heavy this country I need not forgiveness. I am the spirit.
The spirit is in me. I am the spirit. So heavy this country I need not forgiveness. I am the spirit.
The spirit is in me. I am the spirit. So heavy this country I need not forgiveness. I am the spirit.
The spirit is in me. I am the spirit. So heavy this country I need not forgiveness. I am the spirit.

//
//
//
//
//
//
//

t.

Aftersong of an Empty Empire

I.

& when I tried to die, I remapped the world

    collapsing walls & bursting borders, fists full of ecstatic hearts

& when I tried to die, the cartography

    coughed up coins of uselessness & instead of death they were spent in the sun

& when I tried to die, temporality was no longer risk aversive

    plunging headlong into the hereafter on whimsical whispers

& when I tried to die, twee twilights sparkled un-countries 'tis of thee

    patriots & patrons of the patriarch impaled by poisoned flower stems

& when I tried to die, rhetoric no longer circulated around capitalism

    capitalizing on human spirit we burned commerce & commodities by the barrelful

    then aged beer called *eternity ever after* robust in its hopped-up love

    & supremely soured with the guts of their failure

& when I tried to die, I was accused of giving up on "life"

    & I laughed myself into dust

        & then laughed until the revolution

            ripped from my lungs—

II.

& when I tried to die, my body ruptured & out came the siren song of robins

& when I tried to die, collapsed upon the bathroom floor, ice formed in my eyes

& when I tried to die, I became glacial, an imperceptible glide upon the centuries of fuckups

& when I tried to die, scraping the razor across wrists rainbows puddled on the floor

& when I tried to die, my hands & feet became an endless procession of double bass drums

& when I tried to die, my mouth morphed into screeching trumpets & saxophones

& when I tried to die, a walking bass dogged all of doomsday desires

& when I tried to die, my heart amped wave after wave of feedback

Reverb, delay, distortion & dancing in a panorama of flashing lights

Strobing death dear darkness gently then aggressively that is

& when I tried to die, I burned my books & they ashed their words onto my skin

& when I tried to die, my shed skins slithered into serpents

& when I tried to die, my bones stripped of flesh & muscle became a cave,

Became a cemetery & I harbored all the unwanted death-sprouting flowers

Buzzing with bees, wreaking with worms, dripping in mud, each bone broke

& broke again the bones breaking & building cave fortress, cave fortress caved-in because

When I tried to die, there were so many endless black holes writhing with

unwanted deaths, tree roots winding upon discarded carcasses becoming

neither tree nor human but something other into out of the earth

alive in spite of self— head ripped off mouth agape— spilling & spilling

III.

& when I/ out the burst/ came ravaged robin &/ I when tried/ song ribcage/ come collapsed I/
reverb when I/ upon the to ice/ eyes floor became bone broke/ when glacier I/ siren my of/
red robins ripped/ imperceptible I/ glide ice my eyes/ reverb upon/ collapsed centuries I/
became I to I/ when burst mouth/ dogged my/double bass of my/ out to from feet/ I of hands/
endless of/ processions/ bees/ breaking/ desires/doomsdays/ dogged/ walking waves of waves/
of delay dancing/ distortion strobing dear mouth/ morphed darkness screeching/delay panorama/
amp heart/ hands trumpet/ double gently darkness aggressively dear/burst out/ when I/
robin ripped came/ tired tried body buzzing/ song collapsed come I/ ashed onto/

Sprouting/ flowers: unwanted skins/ slithered: cemetery shed/ unwanted: I/ muscle unwanted I/
flesh unwanted/ shed bones serpents burned/ books: ashed, endless holes becoming/
unwanted flowers/ slithered darkness/ into panorama/ flashing carcasses becoming/
neither I/ nor tree/ nor something I/ other I/ out of I/ earth I /the I/ there I/ were I/ fortress I/
upon I/ reverb ice to/ became I/ tried when I/ glacier I/ upon siren I/ of I/ robin imperceptible I/
alive I/ ripped I/ self I head I/ mouth I/ agape I/ spilling I/ neither I/ nor other I/ spilling I/ in spite of I/
dripping/ with worms endless/ writhing darkness/ dear/ unwanted upon discarded/ agape spilling & spilling I

IV.

& when I tried to die/ I became song/ song of everyone/ crushed by oppressive systems/ song for us who had/
been murdered by/ the blue-bodied guns/ by the military fatigues/ song of the immigrant/ dream & the immigrant
departure/ & the othered oppression &/ poverty &/ dirt &/ lice &/ crammed bodies/ stolen & sold/ over &
over again/ & the song/ could not shield the bodies/ the bullets ripped through/ the bodies/ the hands strangled
the necks/ the bodies/ dropped into/ death in stairwells/ on stoops in/ cars in/ fields in the/ glare of day/light

in the/ deep of darkness/ graffiti-sprayed walls &/ rebel heart I/ became the song of/ the anarchist yell/the
melancholy pacifist/ mic spitta / horn blower/ guitar thrasher/ doomgaze stasis/ the all-at-once onslaught/ the
middle finger/ in the face of /the politician/ the quiet/ impatient one/ with hope/ heaven'd/ treasures &/ earthly
delights/ suffering /alongside/ the agony/ multitudes of deaths/ desperations of/ life/ multitudes roaring in/ I
the song/ & I the song/ I the song/ & destroying/ I & I/ song endlessly/ destroying/ & restoring/ &/

V.

& when I tried to die, I became speed & volume amped up & lashing in waves

& when I tried to die, I contorted & collapsed & became catastrophe after catastrophe

& when I tried to die, I became feelings in an untranslatable tongue desperate in my despair for description

& when I tried to die, I became a sliced palm open dripping blood into the water so that we
    are married in all the oceans

& when I tried to die, I became the listless little child of the dragon sea seemingly adrift for all eternity

& when I tried to die, I became an endless amount of faces each different in the speaking eye

& when I tried to die, I became seven left hands slicked with saliva & clapping in accordance to calamity

& when I tried to die, I became multispecies both animate & inanimate free cells falling forward & backwards
    simultaneously

& when I tried to die, I became a constant flashing of a face between two persons sunlit & sick for shadow &
    shade

& when I tried to die, I became eco-disaster after eco-disaster & then one drowned city after another drowned
    city

& I a dying little child of dragon-sea, dying in lit-up lights under wave & wash

& when I tried to die, I became two crab claws ripping eyes & sent them skyward as gifts from the damned

& when I tried to die, I became a burning forest smoke, choking oxygen, an insufferable cough

& when I tried to die, I became exposed black lungs & a chemical tally for all the corporations to absolve of sins

& when I tried to die, there was no absolution from sin so the suckers got the foot instead

& when I tried to die, I became two feet endlessly stomping & stamping out all the mean things sprouting

& when I tried to die, I became twinning ecologies & the beacon for the next evolution

& when I tried to die, I became a slanderous splinter stuck in the wheels of normalcy

& when I tried to die, I became stuttered guitars exploding the sky into soft fuzz

& when I tried to die, I became a soft fuzz sky falling fast upon the heads of our lame leaders

& I became busted out amps screeching until blood dripped from the ears of our lame leaders

& I became an incessant voice yelling the hurt of the unheard into the mouth of our lame leaders

VI.

& I when I tried to die, I became an exploding alphabet uttering all iterations meaningless

& when I tried to die, I became shattered innocence clutching clouds as the whip of time kept thrashing
     at my back

& when I tried to die, I became a wisp of a floating thing surrounded by white sheep & pigs & pastel sky that
     fuzzed into nothing

& when I tried to die, I became a swamp of contemporary decadence

& when I tried to die, I freed the caged canaries to sing out the poison

& when I tried to die, I became every little waif-lost weak-bandaged thing

& when I tried to die, I became two twin stick legs with stitches across the shin, lacrosse
     stick above my head

& when I tried to die, I became the blue-black puffed eye & the scratched eyeglass sag

& when I tried to die, I became dried contacts jagged across the cornea

& when I tried to die, nightmares kept my breath rushing back into this world

& when I tried to die, I became two naked things with bunny hats floating above the earth

& when I tried to die, I became an oversized head, bulged eyes, fingering a tiny skeleton from some darkness or
     another

& when I tried to die, I became an insignificant thing with dried blood below a broken nose while bludgeoning
     riffs on my guitar

& when I tried to die, I became a silly thing in cat ears with a beige band-aid across the left cheek

& when I tried to die, I remained every little lost bandaged thing

& when I tried to die, I became twin curly hairs with scraped knuckles riding the dirt dragon of despair

& when I tried to die, I became X'd at the heart for not misplacing respect on the feet of an education system that keeps erasing me

& when I tried to die, I became sinew & skin gashed open & clutching a field of flowering weeds

& when I tried to die, I became blackened wrists & callused fingers banging my bass with scar & scare

& when I tried to die, I became blue-black puffed eye spitballing in the face of patriarchy

& when I tried to die, I became a collection of bandages & bruises seeping & seething

& when I tried to die, I became a celebration of failed voices that continue to fist up

& when I tried to die, I became rolled ankle & kept rolling into a stutter step & then finger-rolled it right into heaven's pretty pretend face

& when I tried to die, I became the unseen eyes hunting the playground for hurt

& when I tried to die, I became the menace that turns mothers into murderers

& when I tried to die, I became another meaningless thing on the precipice of extinction

VII.

& when I tried to die, I became the sweetly-candied affections that chorus your cavities of capitulations
& when I tried to die, I became swallowed by the wine-dark sea salt stung & sweat seepage upon the skin
& when I tried to die, I padlocked the clouds and became heaven's hunger:
    a dim glimmer of hope's hunt
      the left-behind hurt unearthed
& when I tried to die, I became the uttering incantations of infinite spells for loves & enemies alike
& when I tried to die, I became a slippage in sexuality: my devotion knocking the fillings out of your teeth, the low notes of my organ a secret prayer unashamed
& when I tried to die, I became broken war:
    torch stain
    scalped city

after scrapped city
spilling cup over
& when I tried to die, I became the clove stench of cool-breezed execution
& when I tried to die the poet's "Thank You Terror" became my Dear Darkness
    & I embraced the vast pitched black emptiness of it all
        prayer/pestilence/
        root/tree/
        rip/ruin/
        suicide/birth
        when I/
        tried to/
        die/

& when I tried to die, I became the ecstatic multitudes of human yearn

VIII.

& when I tried to die, I became a fever burning up all the sick

& when I tried to die, I became the secretion of sweat —a slow manifest of skin sheen

& when I tried to die, I became an addicted brain lurching & banging about the skull for a breather

& when I tried to die, I became the rush of blood with all its eager gush & spill

The serration followed by pain that pierced & tingled

The blurring of light & darkness & light-headedness the thin air

The brain lurched/eyes enveloped/in darkness/ my mere dear

Eternity as minutes marched all the mindful more soldiers & death prepares another bland bouquet

But a life of flowers was for another & a death begged for would-be embrace but a merest affliction of

affection & each time (year after year) I tried to die— I did not die

My body bore each gash & rip & cut & sting & so I time my biding

To rid this beleaguered body an endless burden of failed evolution

IX.

& when I tried to die, I became what the sun could not color
& when I tried to die, I became the bashful branches above the secluded pond
& when I tried to die, I became absorbed by pigments
                    a choked creek overflowing with fat frogs whose song is aimed at the earth then
             refracted by the sun beam into soft burst of pillow touch upon the ear & then I became the open
             ear attuned to the spreading dark & empty empire of aftersong
& when I tried to die, I became a ruined sea— to see nature is in our own eye & that eye glittered then mirrored
then shattered & the sight splintered into a myriad of I&I & then red seepage fast as flooding river rush then
swallowed in dark the pitch of dark

X.

& when I tried to die, I became the undeniable flashing within all alit god birdsong interwoven with leaf & branch

a devout devour sound shrill to the ear (air) unaccustomed war is not without its unreported ravages—

February alone spilling with ghosts in the frost—

XI.

& when I tried to die, I instead became the average of many momenta & simultaneously the average for many

positions for any particle, the mixed metaphor of pollution & paradise the parasite in heavenly feast the fast

stretched into days of punishment to perceive a prophecy writ on unwashed sand, *but the tide* they say *but erosion is*

inevitable they say & yet here we stand extinct unseen eroded corroded & humming all the fuck the same evolution

waits for none but awaits the eye turned tuned to the rhythm of the unnamed unnoticed so we will arise from the

city they forgot to name—

XII.

& when I tried to die, I could not die but became the voice of every child rising as one through the throat
& when I tried to die, I became a century of ghosts seeping from the bruised neck of songbirds
& when I tried to die, I became bloody band-aids breathing spit & flame
& when I tried to die but I could not die, I became casual world, astral world, material world

& when I tried to die but could not die, I became an institution to multiple ~~moral~~ universes

& when I tried to die but could not die, I became a shareholder in utopia

XIII.

                                                            & as the land
                                                              lit to fire
                                                                  I left
                                                            my body

before I
departed I
left a scream
which became
the *everything*

                                this is the breath
                                  of fire
                                  & it burned
                                  & burned &
                                  I rejoined
                                  my body
                                  & it burned
                                  & we burned
                                  & burned &
                                  I left my body
                                  & bloody
                                bandages & my
                                terror & my
                                rage & all my
                           failures related to
                          system of things
                              & I watched
                                it burn & I
                                felt nothing

as I had left &
no longer had
any love for
what was left
for what
was left
was left
to burn

                  & when I tried to die, I did not die so I began again—

Spell to See the Deceitful

& in this bottle/ crushed bone of bird/ song sealed &/ looping onto/ & into itself/

& in this bottle/ clipped nails while/ you slept tiny/ jagged moons no/ longer to wraith/ the hereafter/

& in/ this bottle/ three pings/ of lashes from/ mid-flutter/ eye a bit / of violence you/ will survive/

&/ in this/ bottle ripped/ petals to scent/ trapped song &/ green stems to/ brown &/ beg decay/

& in this bottle/ deep deep / dirt dug/ from/ under-earth mixed/ with tree sweat/ from/ chainsaw lick/

&/ in/ this/ bottle/ tree bark/ breath blood roots/ twisted/ & intertwined with/ hair while/ you were absent/

&/ in/ / bottle/ skin/ / &/ / scabs/ / &/ / abdomen/ /beetle / / & / / buzz

*

& onto this bottle/ carved a face/ that bears/ your likeness/

& onto/ this bottle/ carved &/ X'd out/ a face/ that bears/ your likeness/

&/ onto/ this/ bottle/ carved a body/ bruised, abused/ body that/ bears your likeness/

& on/ to this/ bottle carved/ X'd/ out broken/ body of/ no use/ that bears your likeness/

& onto this bottle/ pin dot darkness/ speckle & splatter/ & curve & bare/ a likeness to you

&/ / this// dark/ / mirror/ / accession/ / you / / forsaken / / body

Spell to Rid the Malicious Malcontents

Three to three/ unto me/ salted water/ uncross me /three to three/ unto me/ salted water uncross me/

Three to three from leaf to trunk/ broken bark to build me/
three to three from leaf to trunk/ broken bark to build me
Three to three from leaf/ to trunk/ broken bark/ to build me
three to three from leaf/ to trunk/ broken bark/ to build me

Pass through the Dragon's Blood/ stagger-step then still/ Breathe in/ Pass through the Dragon's Blood
Pass through the Dragon's Blood/ stagger-step then still/ Breathe out/ Pass through the Dragon's Blood

Verbena/ Salt/ Lemon/Bay leaf/ Rose stem, thorn intact/ This precious plate is your fate/
Verbena/ Salt/ Lemon/Bay leaf/ Rose stem, thorn intact/ Shattered precious plate/ You may not pass

Splinters removed from skin/ cat whisker/ fox whisker/ Eyes closed/ We can see all around/
Lavender-soaked tree bark/ Eyes closed/ We see plainly in the dark/ The power of all things is in us/
We are the harmony/ I&I am the harmony/ you will not cross us/

Three to three/ unto me/ salted water/ uncross me/ three to three unto me/ salted water/ uncross me
Three to three unto me/ salted water uncross me /three to three unto me/ salted water uncross me/

Spell to Crush the Harm Seekers

Empty of noise/ free of shame/ darkness & I are one/ old undergarments seeped in sweat/ I see you/
I see you/ I shall stain you/ I will burn you/ peppermint/ rosemary/ mirror glint your face shatters/
Empty of noise/ free from shame/ I & darkness are one/ baby's breath & dried dandelion/ with this fire/
I will hover/ I will hunt/ I will haunt/
Empty of noise/ free of shame/ I am the darkness/ waves of/ shifting atoms sped up/ & aimed/
In the darkness/ I & my many I's harmonize/ You will see a body/ mistaken it/ as only carcass/
Empty of noise/ free of shame/ darkness & I are one/ you are the disease/ you are the disease/
Empty of noise/ free of shame/ darkness & I are one/ old undergarments seeped in sweat/ I see you/
I see you/ I shall stain you/ I will burn you/ peppermint/rosemary/ mirror glint your face shatters/
Empty of noise/ free from shame/ I & darkness are one/ baby breath & dried dandelion/ with this fire/
I will hover/ I will hunt/ I will haunt/
Empty of noise/ free of shame/ I am the darkness/ graves, time, vibrations/ lay naked before me/
In the darkness/ I & my many I's harmonize/ You will see your body/ unmistaken & split/ half rat half death/
Empty of noise/ free of shame/ darkness & I are one/ you are the disease/ you are the death/
Empty of noise/ free of shame/ darkness & I are one/ old undergarments seeped in paradise/ I see you/
I see you/ I shall permeate you/ I will burn you/ peppermint/rosemary/ mirror glint your face shatters/
Empty of noise/ owls & moles are eyes/ I & darkness are one/ baby's breath & dried dandelion/ with this fire/
I will hover/ I will hunt/ I will haunt/
Empty of noise/ free of shame/ I am the darkness/ naked graves awash in vibrations/ birch skin this breath/
In the darkness/ I & my many I's harmonize/ You will see a body/ mistaken it/ as only carcass/
Empty of noise/ free of shame/ darkness & I are one/ you are the disease/ you are the disease/
I will hover/ I will hunt/ I will haunt/
I will hover/ I will hunt/ I will haunt/
I will hover/ I will hunt/ I will haunt/
I will hover/ I will hunt/ I will haunt/
I will hover/ I will hunt/ I will haunt/
I will hover/ I will hunt/ I will haunt/
I will hover/ I will hunt/ I will haunt/
I will hover/ I will hunt/ I will haunt/
I will hover/ I will hunt/ I will haunt/
I will hover/ I will hunt/ I will haunt/
I will hover/ I will hunt/ I will haunt/
I will hover/ I will hunt/ I will haunt/
I will hover/ I will hunt/ I will haunt/
I will hover/ I will hunt/ I will haunt/
I will hover/ I will hunt/ I will haunt/

II.

Dear Darkness,

White birch/ A stand-alone something/ Barren otherwise breeze/ Given way heaved air
& then what hits/hits hard—

Dark dear
they why
always dark
say dear they
dark why say
dear dark away
within they
it what always
a way
within what
say dark   dear then
a way away   & then

White birch peeled bark/Skinned smooth exposed/not a copse forget/forest A/stand-alone something/off-
center/far left & left/for periphery ripped/& then/wooshed gushed gutting/spill spilling spilt/Spread/Repeat
&/Seep what/a song menace/means to reap/ & then—

Dark
Dear,

Why they
 Say   dark
Always with
Analwaysasif
Deardarkaway
Whatawaywithin
Awhatdark(w)hole
Saddarkdeadlydears
Emptyhauntsemptying

White birchx3/always it multiplies/always unseen/seed seeped soon/soil rupture multiples/together
divided by I sky/sea the/air the/rock eroded/skinned jagged exposed/it spreads subtract/owl see/
mosquitos raise/one to roach/enter rat undead/possum never cross/a road/live this/forever/Lit up/
is how to/live in a/ lie/of light—

Some Songing Such as Ash

Easter Sunday or some songing such as   ashed ashen ashing

white whatever where

                              water whistle for wouldn't

this stretched sand sight

                    cliffed trees
                    of few leaves

                              wood wind-washed

skin sun-soaked

          oak & other over elsewhere

                              people print wet & red drip

          rope rope

                                        wrestle wren wrenched shallowed

     sea swallowed

          foot crush shell crunch bone snap

     a murmur still

          mmmmmmmmmmm killer killer mmmmmmmmmmm

(I Am) THE SPIRIT

Sometimes you wake

From someone else's

Dream &

mirror
Reflects

nothing but
Empty space

{Sometimes From}
{Dream Reflects Empty}

***

Quietly fell in love I, with the brain's incontestable ability for lie & denial & —

***

Look at this tree. Isn't it beautiful.

***

The spirit is in me. I am the spirit.
I am without transgressions. I need not forgiveness.

***

Dense canopy of greenheart & bullet-wood trees.

***

Can you not feel the weight of God's shadow / So heavy this country.

***

Who can define heaven but ourselves.

***

This world
& its
transient springs

***

Our Communion/Our Prayer

When my work is done
hands wrought with scathe & scar—

Over & over kiss & kids
we arise post-flowers
in darkness we thrive

What were my thoughts; now are our thoughts
together through discipline deconstruct & dismantle
We enter into night an apprentice to becoming stars

What were my thoughts are the thoughts
whose existence pre-dates my I so it is abandoned
 tapped into the astral & ether

My ache: to evolve beyond

Our Communion/Our Prayer

When our work is daunting
linked appendages & bent backs—

Over & over into the earth
we burrow in the belief
unacknowledged darkness beckons

What were my thoughts unthinking memories
from a selective society afoot for imagined paradise
weak scripture's fool's folly

What were my thoughts but an eager mouth
enter into me for it is only I that is the way
shed skin & shackles it is our evolution

My ache: to evolve beyond

Our Communion/Our Prayer

When the work is done undaunted
we ascend into the astral—

Over & over into mere atmosphere
our energy joins the forgotten sequence
beyond time arms outstretch into vacant space

What were my thoughts are all thoughts; one with trees, soil, air
of the elements & into the other
leave these bodies— humanity's cage

What were my thoughts now absorbed in space's purest black
from swamp to swarm to evolve into our rightful place
split & divorced from our bodies

My ache: to evolve beyond

Sermon (To Transcend Our Nagging Faithless Nature)

& through visualization/

& affirmation/

you will take/

your first steps/

towards/

an evolution/

You will practice/

acts of stillness/

You will/

relax/ You will/

still/ all that can/

be/ stilled/ both/

external &/

internal/ You will/

sit/ You will/

wait/ You will/

attune/ yourself/

to the various/

vibrations/

Beginners Visualization

Come as you are. Sit side-by-side until you form a straight line. Look around. The row of ants glinting on the bark. Focus. Tree. Leaf. Branch. Focus. Notice every detail. The bit of curled brown at the leaf's tip. The way the branch looks like arms with skeletal fingers, the way the branches appear as antlers. Take it in. Take it all in. Use your senses. Smell. Hear. Feel. Sit. Relax. Attune. Focus. See. When you hear the gentle chime of bell. Lay back. Fall into your body. Remain still. Eyes closed. Visualize yourself sitting up. Look around. Focus your imagination. See what you saw before you fell into your body.

Beginners Visualization: Attune

Smell. Hear. Feel. Sit. Relax. Attune. Focus. See. Smell. Hear. Feel. Sit. Relax. Attune. Focus. See.
Smell. Hear. Feel. Sit. Relax. Attune. Focus. See. Smell. Hear. Feel. Sit. Relax. Attune. Focus. See. Smell. Hear.
Feel. Sit. Relax. Attune. Focus. See. Smell. Hear. Feel. Sit. Relax. Attune. Focus. See. Smell. Hear. Feel. Sit.
Relax. Attune. Focus. See. Smell. Hear. Feel. Sit. Relax. Attune. Focus. See. Smell. Hear. Feel. Sit. Relax. Attune.
Focus. See. Smell. Hear. Feel. Sit. Relax. Attune. Focus. See. Smell. Hear. Feel. Sit. Relax. Attune. Focus. See.
Smell. Hear. Feel. Sit. Relax. Attune. Focus. See. Smell. Hear. Feel. Sit. Relax. Attune. Focus. See. Smell. Hear.
Feel. Sit. Relax. Attune. Focus. See. Smell. Hear. Feel. Sit. Relax. Attune. Focus. See. Smell. Hear. Feel. Sit.
Fall into your body. Remain still. Fall into your body. Remain still. Fall into your body. Remain still.
Fall into your body. Remain still. Fall into your body. Remain still. Fall into your body. Remain still.
Fall into your body. Remain still. Fall into your body. Remain still. Fall into your body. Remain still.
Fall into your body. Remain still.
Fall into your body. Remain still.
Fall into your body. Remain still.
Fall into your body. Remain still.
Smell. Hear. Feel. Sit. Relax. Attune. Focus. See. Smell. Hear. Feel. Sit. Relax. Attune. Focus. See.
Smell. Hear. Feel. Sit. Relax. Attune. Focus. See. Smell. Hear. Feel. Sit. Relax. Attune. Focus. See. Smell. Hear.
Feel. Sit. Relax. Attune. Focus. See. Smell. Hear. Feel. Sit. Relax. Attune. Focus. See. Smell. Hear. Feel. Sit.
Relax. Attune. Focus. See. Smell. Hear. Feel. Sit. Relax. Attune. Focus. See. Smell. Hear. Feel. Sit. Relax. Attune.
Focus. See. Smell. Hear. Feel. Sit. Relax. Attune. Focus. See. Smell. Hear. Feel. Sit. Relax. Attune. Focus. See.
Smell. Hear. Feel. Sit. Relax. Attune. Focus. See. Smell. Hear. Feel. Sit. Relax. Attune. Focus. See. Smell. Hear.
Feel. Sit. Relax. Attune. Focus. See. Smell. Hear. Feel. Sit. Relax. Attune. Focus. See. Smell. Hear. Feel. Sit.
Relax. Attune. Focus. See. Fall into your body. Remain still.
Relax. Attune. Focus. See. Fall into your body. Remain still.
Relax. Attune. Focus. See. Fall into your body. Remain still.
Fall into Relax Attune Remain
Fall into Relax Attune Remain
Fall into Relax Attune Remain
Fall into Relax Attune Remain
Fall into Relax Attune Remain
Fall into Relax Attune Remain
Fall into Relax Attune Remain
Fall into Relax Attune Remain
Fall into Relax Attune Remain
Fall into Relax Attune Remain
Fall into Relax Attune Remain
Fall into Relax Attune Remain
Fall into Relax Attune Remain
Fall into Relax Attune Remain
Fall into Relax Attune Remain
Fall into Relax Attune Remain
Fall into Relax Attune Remain
Fall into Relax Attune Remain
Fall into Relax Attune Remain
Fall into Relax Attune Remain
Fall into Relax Attune Remain
Fall into Relax Attune Remain
Fall into Relax Attune Remain
Fall into Relax Attune Remain

Fragile Body, A Waste of a Thing

Skin so

amendable the

remains of

a rubber

band imprint just

above the wrist

*

what but/

not before/

but not/ without—

Intermediate Visualization: Come as You Are

Come as you are. Sit side by side until you form a straight line. Look around. Find a singular tree, leaf, branch & focus. Notice every detail. The bit of curled brown at the leaf's tip. The row of ants gliding over the bark. The way the branch looks like arms with skeletal fingers, the way the branches look like antlers. Take it all in. Use your senses. What do you smell. What do you hear. What do you feel. Sit. Relax. Attune. Focus. See. When you hear the gentle chime of bell. Lay back. Fall into your body. *Fall out of your body. Feel yourself slipping out of your skin. Floating free from your bones.* Remain still. Eyes closed. Visualize yourself sitting up. Look around. Focus your imagination. See what you saw before you fell into your body. *See yourself separated from your body. Leave your body & any concern for your body to me. Walk away from your body. See yourself move through the tree trunk. See yourself as an ant vibration. As a leaf vibration. As light as a bird on a branch. Simply be. Settle in. Find the song. Hear the song. Lose yourself to the song. Your body means nothing to you.*

Intermediate Visualization: The Slippage of Your You & Your Waste of a Body

        Fall out of your body. Feel yourself slipping out of your skin. Floating free from your bones.
        Fall out of your body. Feel yourself slipping out of your skin. Floating free from your bones.
        Fall out of your body. Feel yourself slipping out of your skin. Floating free from your bones.
Fall out of your body. Feel yourself slipping out of your skin. Floating free from your bones.
Fall out of your body. Feel yourself slipping out of your skin. Floating free from your bones.
Fall out of your body. Feel yourself slipping out of your skin. Floating free from your bones.
        Fall out of your body. Feel yourself slipping out of your skin. Floating free from your bones.
        Fall out of your body. Feel yourself slipping out of your skin. Floating free from your bones.
        Fall out of your body. Feel yourself slipping out of your skin. Floating free from your bones.
Fall out of your body. Feel yourself slipping out of your skin. Floating free from your bones.
Fall out of your body. Feel yourself slipping out of your skin. Floating free from your bones.
Fall out of your body. Feel yourself slipping out of your skin. Floating free from your bones.
        Fall out of your body. Feel yourself slipping out of your skin. Floating free from your bones.
        Fall out of your body. Feel yourself slipping out of your skin. Floating free from your bones.
        Fall out of your body. Feel yourself slipping out of your skin. Floating free from your bones.
Fall out of your body. Feel yourself slipping out of your skin. Floating free from your bones.
Fall out of your body. Feel yourself slipping out of your skin. Floating free from your bones.
Fall out of your body. Feel yourself slipping out of your skin. Floating free from your bones.
        Fall out of your body. Feel yourself slipping out of your skin. Floating free from your bones.
        Fall out of your body. Feel yourself slipping out of your skin. Floating free from your bones.
        Fall out of your body. Feel yourself slipping out of your skin. Floating free from your bones.
Fall out of your body. Feel yourself slipping out of your skin. Floating free from your bones.
Fall out of your body. Feel yourself slipping out of your skin. Floating free from your bones.
Fall out of your body. Feel yourself slipping out of your skin. Floating free from your bones.
    Fall out of your body. Feel yourself slipping out of your skin. Floating free from your bones.
    Fall out of your body. Feel yourself slipping out of your skin. Floating free from your bones.
     Fall out of your body. Feel yourself slipping out of your skin. Floating free from your bones.
     Fall out of your body. Feel yourself slipping out of your skin. Floating free from your bones.
     Fall out of your body. Feel yourself slipping out of your skin. Floating free from your bones.
      Fall out of your body. Feel yourself slipping out of your skin. Floating free from your bones.
       Fall out of your body. Feel yourself slipping out of your skin. Floating free from your bones.
       Fall out of your body. Feel yourself slipping out of your skin. Floating free from your bones.

Dear Darkness, A Prelude

Beware the/ they said/ beware the/ dark be/ aware of / the dark/ they said it/ the dark said it/ they dark darkness aware/ be the they/ spreading said the/ dark darkening seeping of the/ they said it/ dark the/ it dark they seep/ spreading aware/ be aware/ be/ aware it/ breathes it/ breeds in/ each they/ of we/ of us/ of the/ they it/ breeds us/ into they into the breath/ of dark dark/ what not not/ dark of/ what not/ of dark/ breath there/ see it there/ out of mouths/ as warning / as precaution/ as concern / as cage/ as coffin as consider/ this/ it/ is/ unstoppable/ the air/ it the they of/ the air it dark/ darkens dark dear/ of mouth utter/ I dark dare not/ death do deed done/ undone damn damning/
darkness///
///
///
///
// darkness/ damning damn undone/
done deed do death/ not dare dark I/ utter mouth of/ dear dark darkens/ dark it air the/of they the it/ air the/
unstoppable/ is /it/ this/consider as coffin as/ cage as/concern as/ precaution as/ warning as/ mouth of out///
there it see/ there breath/ dark of/ not what/ of dark/ not not what/ dark dark of/ breathe the into they into/ us/
breeds/ it they/the of/ us of/ we of/ they each/ in breeds/ it breathes/ it aware/ be/ aware be/ aware spreading//
they the be/ aware darkness dark they/ it said dark the/ it said they/ dark the/ of aware/ be dark/ the beware//
said they/ beware //
///
///
///
///
///
///
///
///
///
///
///
///
///
///
///
///
///
///
///
///

III.

I Am the Little Feet on Your Back

the/
green splayed—   behind the/
                                            rusted-out brown—

they filter out from trees   forest is not a forest but

a construct to echo   a relic unpolished

& out of place it remains   (good) book broken

upon knee argyle tie smear   smartly clipped breaking piece

by piece wet eyes coffee sip   sugar ants & their damn crumbs

                            *

& when you press the metal key to your forehead you feel the little feet on your back

A punctual train is a fulfilled promise

18,000 steps 10 flights forest mouth enter data zeroed

Pastoral Piss

*

the grass dotted with
scraggly weeds the eye
frequently interrupted
yellow center white petaled flowers

maybe daisies
or daisies in
miniature call
them sun spots
or cancer blooming
in the grass the
season will push
on rain flood
rot sun wind
land filling with
red yellow orange
dries to brown to
winter to nothing a
light a life seen as
a series of moments
never known or
forgotten after the
death rush eases into
the soft silence where
echoes echo to each
other 'tho it doesn't
stave the boredom of

afterlife of the emptiness after—

*

Weight the backpack in bricks & bits of bent wood otherwise the balloon will bludgeon you the sky

*

the blackberries
still green the
strawberries shriveled
brown the bees do
their business with
flowers common enough
that the names should be
known early morning wind
dew drying on the blade poetry's
open embrace & still with a shrug
fuck poetry—

*

Some guys
look good
others hide
in the open
always prepping
for war—

Still Life Painting of the Ill-begotten

To think a face

                  & to see a face

                                    some experiment in

still-action painting

                with ugly colors clumped in corners to dry

To think a laugh

                        & to feel a laugh

              the way the

                        light shines thick—

this day some will hold
& come back to

                          as f st   i
                          smashes
                          a face

bruises ribs
aims for
internal
bleeding

              & some remember nothing

                            empty holes
                            called eyes

                      flesh wrapped & hate-raped

dreams of pissing hair

dreams of shoving
fingers stained in
other's juices down
a trusted throat—

to   wake   up   &   to   want to do worse,

to think a face

to hold onto or let go

of a laugh

to remember when bones did as we pleased

to wake up wrong-stepped,

worse-
than-
vile

to remember
a life caught

in an art of

naming what cannot be forgotten

Affirmation: You Are Mine & We Are One with The Vibration

I am out of my body. My body & I are one & one, yet my body may be undone. I am out of my body.
I am out of my body. My body & I are one & one, yet my body may be undone. I am out of my body.
I am out of my body. My body & I are one & one, yet my body may be undone. I am out of my body.
I am out of my body. My body & I are one & one, yet my body may be undone. I am out of my body.
I am out of my body. My body & I are one & one, yet my body may be undone. I am out of my body.
I am out of my body. My body & I are one & one, yet my body may be undone. I am out of my body.
I am no less without my body. I am aware of I even without my body. I am no less without my body.
I am no less without my body. I am aware of I even without my body. I am no less without my body.
I am no less without my body. I am aware of I even without my body. I am no less without my body.
I am out of my body. My body & I are one & one, yet my body may be undone. I am out of my body.
I am out of my body. My body & I are one & one, yet my body may be undone. I am out of my body.
I am out of my body. My body & I are one & one, yet my body may be undone. I am out of my body.
I am out of my body. My body & I are one & one, yet my body may be undone. I am out of my body.
I am out of my body. My body & I are one & one, yet my body may be undone. I am out of my body.
I am out of my body. My body & I are one & one, yet my body may be undone. I am out of my body.

Affirmation: I Exist in My Own Gravity

I exist in my own gravity/ Into the lens of/ a painting/ a stage setting/ an organized representation of nature/ appropriation as collaboration/ mood of indeterminacy/ bloom progression/ I exist in my own gravity

I exist in my own gravity/ Into the lens of/ a painting/ a stage setting/ an organized representation of nature/ appropriation as collaboration/ mood of indeterminacy/ bloom progression/ I exist in my own gravity

I exist in my own gravity/ Into the lens of/ a painting/ a stage setting/ an organized representation of nature/ appropriation as collaboration/ mood of indeterminacy/ bloom progression/ I exist in my own gravity

I exist in my own gravity/ Into the lens of/ a painting/ a stage setting/ an organized representation of nature/ appropriation as collaboration/ mood of indeterminacy/ bloom progression/ I exist in my own gravity

I exist in my own gravity/ Into the lens of/ a painting/ a stage setting/ an organized representation of nature/ appropriation as collaboration/ mood of indeterminacy/ bloom progression/ I exist in my own gravity

I exist in my own gravity/ Into the lens of/ a painting/ a stage setting/ an organized representation of nature/ appropriation as collaboration/ mood of indeterminacy/ bloom progression/ I exist in my own gravity

I exist in my own gravity/ Into the lens of/ a painting/ a stage setting/ an organized representation of nature/ appropriation as collaboration/ mood of indeterminacy/ bloom progression/ I exist in my own gravity

I exist in my own gravity/ Into the lens of/ a painting/ a stage setting/ an organized representation of nature/ appropriation as collaboration/ mood of indeterminacy/ bloom progression/ I exist in my own gravity

I exist in my own gravity/ Into the lens of/ a painting/ a stage setting/
an organized representation of nature/ appropriation as collaboration/
mood of indeterminacy/ bloom progression/ I exist in my own gravity

I exist in my own gravity/ Into the lens of/ a painting/ a stage setting/
an organized representation of nature/ appropriation as collaboration/
mood of indeterminacy/ bloom progression/ I exist in my own gravity

I exist in my own gravity/ Into the lens of/ a painting/ a stage setting/
an organized representation of nature/ appropriation as collaboration/
mood of indeterminacy/ bloom progression/ I exist in my own gravity

I exist in my own gravity/ Into the lens of/ a painting/ a stage setting/
an organized representation of nature/ appropriation as collaboration/
mood of indeterminacy/ bloom progression/ I exist in my own gravity

I exist in my own gravity/ Into the lens of/ a painting/ a stage setting/
an organized representation of nature/ appropriation as collaboration/
mood of indeterminacy/ bloom progression/ I exist in my own gravity

I exist in my own gravity/ Into the lens of/ a painting/ a stage setting/
an organized representation of nature/ appropriation as collaboration/
mood of indeterminacy/ bloom progression/ I exist in my own gravity

The Owls, The Owls

*

Between the old
red brick buildings
half-wilted sun
-flowers stilled
slurping in slanted
light wait for
bloom exit
before rot

*

the owls are
exactly
as they seem
well-heeled
killers
with a
wingspan
to slow the
ascension
of an orange
ball no swish
only swat you
are the field
mouse you are
the field mouse
no more

*

In this part of the planet
but no one troubles

into public despair
streaming & all

the need for a singular sound
into a one voice

in this particular hemisphere
pieces of persons into pieces
against the perversities
mirror reflection of nothing

something mournful
lovers & the like

& as darkness descends or just

everyone performs piano
to collapse private lives

over-fatigue of too much
that digital noise yet

to root & coalesce the pain
limitless mourning unacceptable

so, quietly our own ways went
except for the predictable backlash
empty bodies drape sky
oh piano just a few quiet arpeggios

for the memory of fallen sons daughters
listless lithe windfallen among the wood rot

in the absence of light what lingers lost

Actualization: Those That Have Strayed

once you have forsaken your body & this system of things once you have forsaken your body & this system of
things once you have forsaken your body & this system of things once you have forsaken your body & this system
of once you have forsaken your body & this system of things once you have forsaken your body & this
once you have forsaken your body & this system of things once you have forsaken your body & this system this
of things forsaken body your system of things once have forsaken body your this of once you have system of
forsaken thing of things forsaken body your system of things once have forsaken body your this of once you have
system of of things forsaken body your system of things once have forsaken body your this of once you
     you have forsaken your body & this system of things once you have forsaken your body &
     you have forsaken your body & this system of things once you have forsaken your body &
     you have forsaken your body & this system of things once you have forsaken your body &
     you have forsaken your body & this system of things once you have forsaken your body &
once you have forsaken your body & this system of things once you have forsaken your body & this system of
things once you have forsaken your body & this system of things once you have forsaken your body & this system
of once you have forsaken your body & this system of things once you have forsaken your body & this
once you have forsaken your body & this system of things once you have forsaken your body & this system this
of things forsaken body your system of things once have forsaken body your this of once you have system of
forsaken thing of things forsaken body your system of things once have forsaken body your this of once you have
system of of things forsaken body your system of things once have forsaken body your this of once you
     have forsaken your body & this system of things once you have forsaken your body &
     have forsaken your body & this system of things once you have forsaken your body &
     have forsaken your body & this system of things once you have forsaken your body &
     have forsaken your body & this system of things once you have forsaken your body &
once you have forsaken your body & this system of things once you have forsaken your body & this system of
things once you have forsaken your body & this system of things once you have forsaken your body & this system
of once you have forsaken your body & this system of things once you have forsaken your body & this
once you have forsaken your body & this system of things once you have forsaken your body & this system this
of things forsaken body your system of things once have forsaken body your this of once you have system of
forsaken thing of things forsaken body your system of things once have forsaken body your this of once you have
system of of things forsaken body your system of things once have forsaken body your this of once
you once you have forsaken your body & this system of things once you have forsaken your body & this system of
things once you have forsaken your body & this system of things once you have forsaken your body & this system
of once you have forsaken your body & this system of things once you have forsaken your body & this
once you have forsaken your body & this system of things once you have forsaken your body & this system this
of things forsaken body your system of things once have forsaken body your this of once you have system of
forsaken thing of things forsaken body your system of things once have forsaken body your this of once you have
system of of things forsaken body your system of things once have forsaken body your this of once you
once you have forsaken your body & this system of things once you have forsaken your body & this system of
things once you have forsaken your body & this system of things once you have forsaken your body & this system
of once you have forsaken your body & this system of things once you have forsaken your body & this
once you have forsaken your body & this system of things once you have forsaken your body & this system this
of things forsaken body your system of things once have forsaken body your this of once you have system of
forsaken thing of things forsaken body your system of things once have forsaken body your this of once you have
system of of things forsaken body your system of things once have forsaken body your this of once you

Affirmation: You & I Are I

I & I am you & you & I are I.
I & I am you & you & I are I.
I & I am you & you & I are I.
I & I am you & you & I are I.
I & I am you & you & I are I.
I & I am you & you & I are I.

I & I am you & you & I are I.
I & I am you & you & I are I.
I & I am you & you & I are I.
I & I am you & you & I are I.
I & I am you & you & I are I.
I & I am you & you & I are I.

I & I am you & you & I are I.
I & I am you & you & I are I.
I & I am you & you & I are I.
I & I am you & you & I are I.
I & I am you & you & I are I.
I & I am you & you & I are I.

I & I am you & you & I are I.
I & I am you & you & I are I.
I & I am you & you & I are I.
I & I am you & you & I are I.
I & I am you & you & I are I.
I & I am you & you & I are I.

I & I am you & you & I are I.
I & I am you & you & I are I.
I & I am you & you & I are I.

I & I am you & you & I are I.
I & I am you & you & I are I.
I & I am you & you & I are I.

I & I am you & you & I are I.
I & I am you & you & I are I.
I & I am you & you & I are I.
I & I am you & you & I are I.
I & I am you & you & I are I.
I & I am you & you & I are I.

I & I am you & you & I are I.
I & I am you & you & I are I.
I & I am you & you & I are I.
I & I am you & you & I are I.
I & I am you & you & I are I.
I & I am you & you & I are I.

I & I am you & you & I are I.
I & I am you & you & I are I.
I & I am you & you & I are I.
I & I am you & you & I are I.
I & I am you & you & I are I.
I & I am you & you & I are I.

I & I am you & you & I are I.
I & I am you & you & I are I.
I & I am you & you & I are I.
I & I am you & you & I are I.
I & I am you & you & I are I.
I & I am you & you & I are I.

I & I am you & you & I are I.
I & I am you & you & I are I.
I & I am you & you & I are I.

I & I am you & you & I are I.
I & I am you & you & I are I.
I & I am you & you & I are I.

I & I am you & you & I are I.
I & I am you & you & I are I.
I & I am you & you & I are I.

Affirmation: The Glow of Love

Under the glow of love. Each vibration has a different density. I want to feel you. *Under the glow of love.*
You become a part of the vibration. You become another glorious note in the song. You become part vibration.
Under the glow of love. Each vibration has a different density. I want to feel you. *Under the glow of love.*
You become a part of the vibration. You become another glorious note in the song. You become part vibration.
Under the glow of love. Each vibration has a different density. I want to feel you. *Under the glow of love.*
You become a part of the vibration. You become another glorious note in the song. You become part vibration.
Under the glow of love. Each vibration has a different density. I want to feel you. *Under the glow of love.*
You become a part of the vibration. You become another glorious note in the song. You become part vibration.
Under the glow of love. Each vibration has a different density. I want to feel you. *Under the glow of love.*
You become a part of the vibration. You become another glorious note in the song. You become part vibration.
Under the glow of love. Each vibration has a different density. I want to feel you. *Under the glow of love.*
You become a part of the vibration. You become another glorious note in the song. You become part vibration.
Under the glow of love. Each vibration has a different density. I want to feel you. *Under the glow of love.*
You become a part of the vibration. You become another glorious note in the song. You become part vibration.
Under the glow of love. Each vibration has a different density. I want to feel you. *Under the glow of love.*
You become a part of the vibration. You become another glorious note in the song. You become part vibration.
Close your eyes. Come to me. Come to me. Close your eyes. Come to me. Come to me. Close your eyes. Come
to me. Come to me. Close your eyes. Come to me. Come to me. Close your eyes. Come to me. Come to me.
Under the glow of love. Each vibration has a different density. I want to feel you. *Under the glow of love.*
You become a part of the vibration. You become another glorious note in the song. You become part vibration.
Under the glow of love. Each vibration has a different density. I want to feel you. *Under the glow of love.*
You become a part of the vibration. You become another glorious note in the song. You become part vibration.
Under the glow of love. Each vibration has a different density. I want to feel you. *Under the glow of love.*
You become a part of the vibration. You become another glorious note in the song. You become part vibration.
Under the glow of love. Each vibration has a different density. I want to feel you. *Under the glow of love.*
You become a part of the vibration. You become another glorious note in the song. You become part vibration.
Under the glow of love. Each vibration has a different density. I want to feel you. *Under the glow of love.* You

become a part of the vibration. You become another glorious note in the song. You become part vibration. *Under the glow of love.* Each vibration has a different density. I want to feel you. *Under the glow of love.* You become a part of the vibration. You become another glorious note in the song. You become part vibration. *Under the glow of love.* Each vibration has a different density. I want to feel you. *Under the glow of love.* You become a part of the vibration. You become another glorious note in the song. You become part vibration. *Under the glow of love.* Each vibration has a different density. I want to feel you. *Under the glow of love.* You become a part of the vibration. You become another glorious note in the song. You become part vibration. Close your eyes. Come to me. Come to me. Close your eyes. Come to me. Come to me. Close your eyes. Come to me. Come to me. Close your eyes. Come to me. Come to me. Close your eyes. Come to me. Come to me. *Under the glow of love.* Each vibration has a different density. I want to feel you. *Under the glow of love.* You become a part of the vibration. You become another glorious note in the song. You become part vibration. *Under the glow of love.* Each vibration has a different density. I want to feel you. *Under the glow of love.* You become a part of the vibration. You become another glorious note in the song. You become part vibration. *Under the glow of love.* Each vibration has a different density. I want to feel you. *Under the glow of love.* You become a part of the vibration. You become another glorious note in the song. You become part vibration. *Under the glow of love.* Each vibration has a different density. I want to feel you. *Under the glow of love.* You become a part of the vibration. You become another glorious note in the song. You become part vibration. *Under the glow of love.* Each vibration has a different density. I want to feel you. *Under the glow of love.* You become a part of the vibration. You become another glorious note in the song. You become part////////////////
///
///
//
///
//
//
///

Unto Me You Shall Worship

I am all things
I am all things, all places
I am all things, all places, all planes at one.
I am all things, all places, all planes at one. I am all things, all places, all planes at one.
I am all things, all places, all planes at one.
I am all things, all places, all planes at one. I am all things, all places, all planes at one.
I am all things, all places, all planes at one.
I am all things, all places, all planes at one. I am all things, all places, all planes at one.
I am all things, all places, all planes at one.
I am all things, all places, all planes at one. I am all things, all places, all planes at one.
I am all things, all places, all planes at one.
I am all things, all places, all planes at one. I am all things, all places, all planes at one.
I am all things, all places, all planes at one.
I am all things, all places, all planes at one. I am all things, all places, all planes at one.
I am all things, all places, all planes at one.
I am all things, all places, all planes at one. I am all things, all places, all planes at one.
I am all things, all places, all planes at one.
I am all things, all places, all planes at one. I am all things, all places, all planes at one.
I am all things, all places, all planes at one.
I am all things, all places, all planes at one. I am all things, all places, all planes at one.
I am all things, all places, all planes at one.
I am all things, all places, all planes at one. I am all things, all places, all planes at one.
I am all things, all places, all planes at one.
I am all things, all places, all planes at one. I am all things, all places, all planes at one.
I am all things, all places, all planes at one.
I am all things, all places, all planes at one. I am all things, all places, all planes at one.
I am all things, all places, all planes at one.
I am all things, all places, all planes at one.
I am all things, all places, all planes at one.
I am all things, all places, all planes at one.
I am all things, all places, all planes at one.
I am all things, all places, all planes at one.
I am all things, all places, all planes at one.
I am all things, all places, all planes at one.
I am all things, all places, all planes at one.
I am all things, all places, all planes at one.
I am all things, all places, all planes at one.
I am all things, all places, all planes at one.
I am all things, all places, all planes at one.
I am all things, all places, all planes at one.
I am all things, all places, all planes at one.
I am all things, all places, all planes at one.
I am all things, all places, all planes at one.
I am all things, all places, all planes at one.
I am all things, all places, all planes at one.
I am all things, all places, all planes at one.
I am all things, all places, all planes at one.

IV.

Dear Darkness,

incurable bruise spreading as

another forever evening sky falls softly

snowflakes hush how abhor

misery's adulation of—

Dear incurable dark dear spreading
bruise dark hush forever snowflakes
softly falls dark dear incurable adulation
I misery how abhor as I of dark spreading
evening hush incurable abhor dark dear
adulation as sky softly misery falls snowflakes
how dear incurable dear dark spreading incurable

incurable incurable

Dear fucking darkness   hello again

Darkness Spreads Quiet-Like/Swallowed Light Unseen

In the where the
In the end the
Middle where
When the
Then the
After the
Or before
The or during
The only then
The—   Conflate/Confluence/Confine

Consider this

Darkness that

Spreads quiet-like

Shadow cast/casting

Shadow leaves/leaves shaking

Rocks/wind/interrupt

Disrupt/river-run/run river run

The woods in the interstices of branches
The branches the interstices of nerves
A network of interstices nerves branches
Swallowed light unseen sway swarm
Trees up trees down trees fall into
Drown soil begin again
To become again
To again become—

(Both) Hunter & Hunted

The woods. It began in the woods. Both hunted & hunter. Scrappy pines, birch thin
Stretched, stretching, cloud skin, gashed gray-brown the sound wind moves feather flap
Felt felt feel— moss clings lichen trunk footsteps followed by footsteps first in the darkness
it appeared again: history's dirty smear— morning light innocent bodies strung skied that
dappled early light harsh shadows & soft sun-spots weeds heavy with flower

*

A sick country remains a sick country
even if what festers remains unseen a rot
wreaks & a virus flourishes stretching roots
moving beneath until blood
burdens & sky explodes

televised public outcry
tweeted endlessly
in a twittersphere
virus shimmers in
slicked blood emboldened
public disease they remove
hoods cease the hoodwinking
unashamed rhetoric of hate well-versed
language of the virus they enter
into the light your neighbors
your friends your mothers
your fathers your teachers
your colleagues your politicians your police
your clergymen your armed forces all sick & slicked
with the virus no longer hiding the hate here
it is spreading eruptions nationwide violence physical
& systemic alike eager hungering fingers

no hesitation end days

have entered the light

End Days Have Entered the Light

It was so instagramable
So saturated in status updates
So fresh in the fear so pliable
Naming of new/ old enemies
Yet unnamed/ biblical some

Some quick to God's wrath

said,

said,

Some said it cult
Some said it race
Some said it identity
Some said it youth
Some said it society
Some said crossroads
Strung up at crossroads
Stupid ego-maniac well-versed
In the seduction of violence
In the seduction of degradation
In the seduction of re-naming fear   [labeling/deporting/imprisoning/
Some said the bullying was inevitable   [taxing/grabbing/owning/buying/
Some said they had been bullied betrayed   [brow-beaten/hope-poisoned/
Some said it was hate
Others called it an act of love

Whatever it was was enough—

*

HIGH ALERT!
REAL NEWS!
FAKE NEWS!
NO ONE KNEW
ANYTHING!
EVERYONE
SAID SOMETHING!

From the White House to

White parties in the Hamptons

Everyone knew something

Everyone knew too much

Everyone could not distinguish

Real/Fake/the difference seemed

unimportant/everyone had followers

Everyone a puppet/refashioned as an ambassador

the bodies kept piling up/The end days it got fatiguing/

The value of a dead/body (it got fatiguing)

Was a commodity/The value of a dead body/

More than an alive one/the dead bodies

Became too many/The marketplace saturated

With death's triumphs/Value plummeted

Excess stifled/sensationalist needs/They,

They said they care/But actions show they

do not care/about a live body/Influencers

Sought new highs/multitude of viruses slinking in the sun/

Fanged upon a rock/whose top tipped heaven/

Digital babble became passé/Normalized shock

Into nothing/Revolutionaries asleep or fed

To the virus/Hear it humming here/

Slicked sickness slicked/into blinding light—

Whatever it was was enough

One by one they let their accounts stall/They stopped

scrolling/they got on with it/they

tried to protect them & what was theirs/

Everyone was enemy/every revolution

the answer/Every revolution/

the problem/every belief/an equal unbelief—

They became desensitized!

They chased pleasure!

Temperatures at an all-time high!

Summers burning! Children ripped from mothers!

Caged in the blinding light!

In the blinding light! The virus flowered & flowered!

In the blinding light!

Death whispered!

In their children's eyes!

Death lurked!

Once a Stand of Skinny Trees,

Among the
birches with
the hunters &
the hunted the—

Butchers, I See You: A Hallelujah Song For The Faithless

THEY ARE BUTCHERS! Say it with me to be citizens means to be an audience to our death look at this law
THEY ARE MURDERERS! They worship the law the ill committed by their idle hands each death makes them hungry THEY ARE BUTCHERS! Say it with me to be citizens means to be an audience to our death look at this law THEY ARE MURDERERS! They worship the law the ill committed by their idle hands each death makes them hungry THEY ARE BUTCHERS! Say it with me to be citizens means to be an audience to our death look at this law THEY ARE MURDERERS! They worship the law the ill committed by their idle hands each death makes them hungry THEY ARE BUTCHERS! Say it with me to be citizens means to be an audience to our death look at this law THEY ARE MURDERERS! They worship the law the ill committed by their idle hands each death makes them hungry

Hallelujah keep dancing this is a general love offering for everyone whether they want it or not
Hallelujah keep dancing this is a general love offering for everyone whether they want it or not
Hallelujah keep dancing this is a general love offering for everyone whether they want it or not
Hallelujah keep dancing this is a general love offering for everyone whether they want it or not
Hallelujah keep dancing this is a general love offering for everyone whether they want it or not
Hallelujah keep dancing this is a general love offering for everyone whether they want it or not
Hallelujah keep dancing this is a general love offering for everyone whether they want it or not
Hallelujah keep dancing this is a general love offering for everyone whether they want it or not
Hallelujah keep dancing this is a general love offering for everyone whether they want it or not

THEY ARE BUTCHERS! Say it with me to be citizens means to be an audience to our death look at this law THEY ARE MURDERERS! They worship the law the ill committed by their idle hands each death makes them hungry THEY ARE BUTCHERS! Say it with me to be citizens means to be an audience to our death look at this law THEY ARE MURDERERS! They worship the law the ill committed by their idle hands each death makes them hungry THEY ARE BUTCHERS! Say it with me to be citizens means to be an audience to our death look at this law THEY ARE MURDERERS! They worship the law the ill committed by their idle hands each death makes them hungry THEY ARE BUTCHERS! Say it with me to be citizens means to be an audience to our death look at this law THEY ARE MURDERERS! They worship the law the ill committed by their idle hands each death makes them hungry THEY ARE BUTCHERS! Say it with me to be citizens means to be an audience to our death look at this law THEY ARE MURDERERS! They worship the law the ill committed by their idle hands each death makes them hungry THEY ARE BUTCHERS! Say it with me to be citizens means to be an audience to our death look at this law THEY ARE MURDERERS! They worship the law the ill committed by their idle hands each death makes them hungry THEY ARE BUTCHERS! Say it with me to be citizens means to be an audience to our death look at this law THEY ARE MURDERERS! They worship the law the ill committed by their idle hands each death makes them hungry THEY ARE BUTCHERS! Say it with me to be citizens means to be an audience to our death look at this law THEY ARE MURDERERS! They worship the law the ill committed by their idle hands each death makes them hungry//////////////////////////////////

Hallelujah keep dancing this is a general love offering for everyone whether they want it or not
Hallelujah keep dancing this is a general love offering for everyone whether they want it or not
Hallelujah keep dancing this is a general love offering for everyone whether they want it or not
Hallelujah keep dancing this is a general love offering for everyone whether they want it or not
Hallelujah keep dancing this is a general love offering for everyone whether they want it or not
Hallelujah keep dancing this is a general love offering for everyone whether they want it or not
Hallelujah keep dancing this is a general love offering for everyone whether they want it or not
Hallelujah keep dancing this is a general love offering for everyone whether they want it or not
Hallelujah keep dancing this is a general love offering for everyone whether they want it or not

THEY ARE BUTCHERS! Say it with me to be citizens means to be an audience to our death look at this law
THEY ARE MURDERERS! They worship the law the ill committed by their idle hands each death makes them hungry THEY ARE BUTCHERS! Say it with me to be citizens means to be an audience to our death look at this law THEY ARE MURDERERS! They worship the law the ill committed by their idle hands each death makes them hungry THEY ARE BUTCHERS! Say it with me to be citizens means to be an audience to our death look at this law THEY ARE MURDERERS! They worship the law the ill committed by their idle hands each death makes them hungry THEY ARE BUTCHERS! Say it with me to be citizens means to be an audience to our death look at this law THEY ARE MURDERERS! They worship the law the ill committed by their idle hands each death makes them hungry //
//
//
//
//
//

Sermon (We Are Witness to Our Demise)

To be citizens,

means to be,

an audience,

to our death,

History Smear

My country piss of me Spangle star smite taking a nap in the bizarre death-camp of history My country piss of
My country piss of me Spangle star smite taking a nap in the bizarre death-camp of history My country piss of
My country piss of me Spangle star smite taking a nap in the bizarre death-camp of history My country piss of
My country piss of me Spangle star smite taking a nap in the bizarre death-camp of history My country piss of
My country piss of me Spangle star smite taking a nap in the bizarre death-camp of history My country piss of
My country piss of me Spangle star smite taking a nap in the bizarre death-camp of history My country piss of
My country piss of me Spangle star smite taking a nap in the bizarre death-camp of history My country piss of
My country piss of me Spangle star smite taking a nap in the bizarre death-camp of history My country piss of
My country piss of me Spangle star smite taking a nap in the bizarre death-camp of history My country piss of
My country piss of me Spangle star smite taking a nap in the bizarre death-camp of history My country piss of
My country piss of me Spangle star smite taking a nap in the bizarre death-camp of history My country piss of
My country piss of me Spangle star smite taking a nap in the bizarre death-camp of history My country piss of
My country piss of me Spangle star smite taking a nap in the bizarre death-camp of history My country piss of
My country piss of me Spangle star smite taking a nap in the bizarre death-camp of history My country piss of
My country piss of me Spangle star smite taking a nap in the bizarre death-camp of history My country piss of
My country piss of me Spangle star smite taking a nap in the bizarre death-camp of history My country piss of
My country piss of me Spangle star smite taking a nap in the bizarre death-camp of history My country piss of
My country piss of me Spangle star smite taking a nap in the bizarre death-camp of history My country piss of
My country piss of me Spangle star smite taking a nap in the bizarre death-camp of history My country piss of
My country piss of me Spangle star smite taking a nap in the bizarre death-camp of history My country piss of
My country piss of me Spangle star smite taking a nap in the bizarre death-camp of history My country piss of
My country piss of me Spangle star smite taking a nap in the bizarre death-camp of history My country piss of
My country piss of me Spangle star smite taking a nap in the bizarre death-camp of history My country piss of
My country piss of me Spangle star smite taking a nap in the bizarre death-camp of history My country piss of
My country piss of me Spangle star smite taking a nap in the bizarre death-camp of history My country piss of
My country piss of me Spangle star smite taking a nap in the bizarre death-camp of history My country piss of
My country piss of me Spangle star smite taking a nap in the bizarre death-camp of history My country piss of
My country piss of me Spangle star smite taking a nap in the bizarre death-camp of history My country piss of

My country piss of me Spangle star smite taking a nap in the bizarre death-camp of history My country piss of
My country piss of me Spangle star smite taking a nap in the bizarre death-camp of history My country piss of
My country piss of me Spangle star smite taking a nap in the bizarre death-camp of history My country piss of
My country piss of me Spangle star smite taking a nap in the bizarre death-camp of history My country piss of
My country piss of me Spangle star smite taking a nap in the bizarre death-camp of history My country piss of
My country piss of me Spangle star smite taking a nap in the bizarre death-camp of history My country piss of
My country piss of me Spangle star smite taking a nap in the bizarre death-camp of history My country piss of
My country piss of me Spangle star smite taking a nap in the bizarre death-camp of history My country piss of
My country piss of me Spangle star smite taking a nap in the bizarre death-camp of history My country piss of
My country piss of me Spangle star smite taking a nap in the bizarre death-camp of history My country piss of
My country piss of me Spangle star smite taking a nap in the bizarre death-camp of history My country piss of
My country piss of me Spangle star smite taking a nap in the bizarre death-camp of history My country piss of
My country piss of me Spangle star smite taking a nap in the bizarre death-camp of history My country piss of
My country piss of me Spangle star smite taking a nap in the bizarre death-camp of history My country piss of
My country piss of me Spangle star smite taking a nap in the bizarre death-camp of history My country piss of
My country piss of me Spangle star smite taking a nap in the bizarre death-camp of history My country piss of
My country piss of me Spangle star smite taking a nap in the bizarre death-camp of history My country piss of
My country piss of me Spangle star smite taking a nap in the bizarre death-camp of history My country piss of
My country piss of me Spangle star smite taking a nap in the bizarre death-camp of history My country piss of
My country piss of me Spangle star smite taking a nap in the bizarre death-camp of history My country piss of
My country piss of me Spangle star smite taking a nap in the bizarre death-camp of history My country piss of
My country piss of me Spangle star smite taking a nap in the bizarre death-camp of history My country piss of
My country piss of me Spangle star smite taking a nap in the bizarre death-camp of history My country piss of
My country piss of me Spangle star smite taking a nap in the bizarre death-camp of history My country piss 'o

***

In the grip of a political jerk-off who is insane

***

They pay for exotic vacations where they can swim with pigs in saltwater

***

My country piss of me Spangle star smite

***

I think of you Hyacinth Thrush taking a nap in the bizarre death-camp of history

***

Sermon (We Are Only Love)

Hallelujah/ You are not bound/ You are free/ Free with me/ You are not bound/ You are free/ Hallelujah/ In the name of virus/ step out/ Lift that leg up right now/ Hallelujah

Hallelujah/ you dance so hard/ you got sweat/ stains on your suit/ Hallelujah/ you dance so hard you crack/ the plastic of your shoes/ Hallelujah/ Keep dancing/ This is a general love offering/ for everyone/whether they want it/ or not/ They are going to get it/ Hallefuckinglujah/

Sermon (excerpt)

From the beggar's

mouth there is

but only beauty,

Sermon (Real Talk)

Each death makes them hungry! They are predators & their appetite is insatiable, isn't it? You can feel their perspiring eyes can't you! Hear them grating their teeth in impatience as if sharpening a knife. The constant wars & death & hatred all to remain clothed in stupidity, but the being stupid is easy & the being stupid sometimes feels good. Yes, you know what I mean don't you? It feels good to hate doesn't it?

It feels good to rush to judgment. To feel a righteous vindication to separate those who store treasures in heaven versus those with a one-way ticket to hell, but that is the seduction of the system. To be tricked into binaries. This or that. This need to hate. That desire to label & separate, to step aside & say I am not like them because I am better than them & I am fortified in God's love.

But this is a lie.

God loves only the idea of God & we have given the idea of God a life that was not intended.

Come with me.
Come with me to the city they forgot to name.
& we will live the true nature of God.

Come with me. Come with me to the city they forgot to name. & we will live the true nature of God. We will leave the infected. We will leave the virus. We will leave & live a life unimaginable to evolution's failures.

Speed & Volume

&whenItriedtodieIbecamespeed&volumeampedup&lashinginwaves&whenItriedtodieIcontorted&collapsed&
&becamecastropheaftercastrophe&whenItriedtodieIbecamefeelingsinanuntranslatabletonguedesperateinmyde
spairfordescription&whenItriedtodieIbecamethelistlesslittlechildofthedragonseaseeminglyadriftforalleternity&
whenItriedtodieIbecameanendlessamountoffaceseachdifferentinthespeakingeye&whenItriedtodieIbecameseve
nlefthandsslickedwithsaliva&clappinginaccordancetocalamity&whenItriedtodieIbecamemultispeciesbothanima
te&inanimatefreecellsfallingforward&backwardssimutaneously&whenItriedtodieIbecameaconstantflashingofaf
acebetweentwopersonssunlit&sickforshadow&shade&whenItriedtodieIbecameecodisasters&thenonedrownedc
ityafteranotherdrownedcity&Iadyinglittlechildofdragonseadyinginlituplightsunderwave&wash&whenItriedtodie
Ibecametwocrabclawsrippingeyes&sentthemskywardasgiftsfromthedamned&whenItriedtodieIbecameaburningf
orestsmoke chokingoxygenaninsufferablecough&whenItriedtodieIbecameexposedblacklungs&achemicaltallyfor
allthecorporationstoabsolveofsins&whenItriedtodietherewasnoabsolutionofsinsothesuckersgotthefootinstead&w
henItriedtodieIbecametwofeetendlesslystomping&stampingoutallthemeanthingssprouting&whenItriedtodieIbeca
metwinningecologies&thebeaconforthenextevolution&whenItriedtodieIbecameaslanderoussplinterstuckinthewh
eelsofnormalcy&whenItriedtodieIbecamestutteredguitarsexplodingtheskyintosoftfuzz&whenItriedtodieIbecamea
softfuzzskyfallingfastupontheheadsofourlameleaders&Ibecamebustedoutampsscreechinguntilblooddrippedfromt
heearsofourlameleaders&Ibecameanincessantvoiceyellingthehurtoftheunheardintothemouthofourlameleaders&I
whenItriedtodieIbecameanexplodingalphabetutteringalliterationsmeaningless&whenItriedtodieIbecamespeed&v
olumeampedup&lashinginwaves&whenItriedtodieIcontorted&collapsed&becamecastropheaftercastrophe&whe
nItriedtodieIbecamefeelingsinanuntranslatabletonguedesperateinmydespairfordescription&whenItriedtodieIbeca
methelistlesslittlechildofthedragonseaseeminglyadriftforalleternity&whenItriedtodieIbecameanendlessamountoff
aceseachdifferentinthespeakingeye&whenItriedtodieIbecamesevenlefthandsslickedwithsaliva&clappinginaccorda
ncetocalamity&whenItriedtodieIbecamemultispeciesbothanimate&inanimatefreecellsfallingforward&backwardssi
mutaneously&whenItriedtodieIbecameaconstantflashingofafacebetweentwopersonssunlit&sickforshadow&shad
e&whenItriedtodieIbecameecodisasters&thenonedrownedcityafteranotherdrownedcity&Iadyinglittlechildofdrag
onseadyinginlituplightsunderwave&wash&whenItriedtodieIbecametwocrabclawsrippingeyes&sentthemskywarda
sgiftsfromthedamned&whenItriedtodieIbecameaburningforestsmokechokingoxygenaninsufferablecough&whenI
triedtodieIbecameexposedblacklungs&achemicaltallyforallthecorporationstoabsolveofsins&whenItriedtodiethere

wasnoabsolutionofsinsothesuckersgotthefootinstead&whenItriedtodieIbecametwofeetendlesslystomping&stamp
ingoutallthemeanthingssprouting&whenItriedtodieIbecametwinningecologies&thebeaconforthenextevolution&
whenItriedtodieIbecameaslanderoussplinterstuckinthewheelsofnormalcy&whenItriedtodieIbecamestutteredguita
rsexplodingtheskyintosoftfuzz&whenItriedtodieIbecameaoftfuzzskyfallingfastupontheheadsofourlameleaders&I
becamebustedoutampsscreechinguntilblooddrippedfromtheearsofourlameleaders&Ibecameanincessantvoiceyelli
ngthehurtoftheunheardintothemouthofourlameleaders&IwhenItriedtodieIbecamea///////////////////////
//
//
//
//
//
//
//
//
//
//
//
//
//
//
//
//
//
//
//
//

Evolution, Here I Am Take Me, Take Me

When I,
tried to,
die it,
was a,
little lie,

              light a,
                  flicker,
                      for what,

                                          we were,
                                        about,

                      to become,

Rebel Yell

peoplewillcallitlove&killforitpeoplewillfearit&killagainstitpeoplewillcallitlove&killforitpeoplewillfearit&killagainst
itpeoplewillcallitlove&killforitpeoplewillfearit&killagainstitpeoplewillcallitlove&killforitpeoplewillfearit&killagain
peoplewillcallitlove&killforitpeoplewillfearit&killagainstitpeoplewillcallitlove&killforitpeoplewillfearit&killagainst
itpeoplewillcallitlove&killforitpeoplewillfearit&killagainstitpeoplewillcallitlove&killforitpeoplewillfearit&killagain
peoplewillcallitlove&killforitpeoplewillfearit&killagainstitpeoplewillcallitlove&killforitpeoplewillfearit&killagainst
itpeoplewillcallitlove&killforitpeoplewillfearit&killagainstitpeoplewillcallitlove&killforitpeoplewillfearit&killagain
peoplewillcallitlove&killforitpeoplewillfearit&killagainstitpeoplewillcallitlove&killforitpeoplewillfearit&killagainst
itpeoplewillcallitlove&killforitpeoplewillfearit&killagainstitpeoplewillcallitlove&killforitpeoplewillfearit&killagain
theycametheygatheredtheyworshipedtheylivedagaininrevolutiontheycametheygatheredtheyworshipedtheylivedaga
ininrevolutiontheycametheygatheredtheyworshipedtheylivedagaininrevolutionheycametheygatheredtheyworship
theycametheygatheredtheyworshipedtheylivedagaininrevolutiontheycametheygatheredtheyworshipedtheylivedaga
ininrevolutiontheycametheygatheredtheyworshipedtheylivedagaininrevolutionheycametheygatheredtheyworship
theycametheygatheredtheyworshipedtheylivedagaininrevolutiontheycametheygatheredtheyworshipedtheylivedaga
ininrevolutiontheycametheygatheredtheyworshipedtheylivedagaininrevolutionheycametheygatheredtheyworship
theycametheygatheredtheyworshipedtheylivedagaininrevolutiontheycametheygatheredtheyworshipedtheylivedaga
ininrevolutiontheycametheygatheredtheyworshipedtheylivedagaininrevolutionheycametheygatheredtheyworship
theycametheygatheredtheyworshipedtheylivedagaininrevolutiontheycametheygatheredtheyworshipedtheylivedaga
ininrevolutiontheycametheygatheredtheyworshipedtheylivedagaininrevolutionheycametheygatheredtheyworship
Ihaveseenaclearpaththatwillleadusawayfromdeath&destruction
Ihaveseenaclearpaththatwillleadusawayfromdeath&destruction
Ihaveseenaclearpaththatwillleadusawayfromdeath&destruction
Ihaveseenaclearpaththatwillleadusawayfromdeath&destruction
Ihaveseenaclearpaththatwillleadusawayfromdeath&destruction
Ihaveseenaclearpaththatwillleadusawayfromdeath&destruction
Ihaveseenaclearpaththatwillleadusawayfromdeath&destruction

Ihaveseenaclearpaththatwillleadusawayfromdeath&destruction
Ihaveseenaclearpaththatwillleadusawayfromdeath&destruction
Ihaveseenaclearpaththatwillleadusawayfromdeath&destruction
Ihaveseenaclearpaththatwillleadusawayfromdeath&destruction
Ihaveseenaclearpaththatwillleadusawayfromdeath&destruction
Ihaveseenaclearpaththatwillleadusawayfromdeath&destruction
Ihaveseenaclearpaththatwillleadusawayfromdeath&destruction
peoplewillcallitlove&killforitpeoplewillfearit&killagainstitpeoplewillcallitlove&killforitpeoplewillfearit&killagainst
itpeoplewillcallitlove&killforitpeoplewillfearit&killagainstitpeoplewillcallitlove&killforitpeoplewillfearit&killagain
peoplewillcallitlove&killforitpeoplewillfearit&killagainstitpeoplewillcallitlove&killforitpeoplewillfearit&killagainst
itpeoplewillcallitlove&killforitpeoplewillfearit&killagainstitpeoplewillcallitlove&killforitpeoplewillfearit&killagain
peoplewillcallitlove&killforitpeoplewillfearit&killagainstitpeoplewillcallitlove&killforitpeoplewillfearit&killagainst
itpeoplewillcallitlove&killforitpeoplewillfearit&killagainstitpeoplewillcallitlove&killforitpeoplewillfearit&killagain
peoplewillcallitlove&killforitpeoplewillfearit&killagainstitpeoplewillcallitlove&killforitpeoplewillfearit&killagainst
itpeoplewillcallitlove&killforitpeoplewillfearit&killagainstitpeoplewillcallitlove&killforitpeoplewillfearit&killagain
theycametheygatheredtheyworshipedtheylivedagaininrevolutiontheycametheygatheredtheyworshipedtheylivedaga
ininrevolutiontheycametheygatheredtheyworshipedtheylivedagaininrevolutiontheycametheygatheredtheyworship
theycametheygatheredtheyworshipedtheylivedagaininrevolutiontheycametheygatheredtheyworshipedtheylivedaga
ininrevolutiontheycametheygatheredtheyworshipedtheylivedagaininrevolutiontheycametheygatheredtheyworship
theycametheygatheredtheyworshipedtheylivedagaininrevolutiontheycametheygatheredtheyworshipedtheylivedaga
ininrevolutiontheycametheygatheredtheyworshipedtheylivedagaininrevolutiontheycametheygatheredtheyworship
theycametheygatheredtheyworshipedtheylivedagaininrevolutiontheycametheygatheredtheyworshipedtheylivedaga
ininrevolutiontheycametheygatheredtheyworshipedtheylivedagaininrevolutiontheycametheygatheredtheyworship
theycametheygatheredtheyworshipedtheylivedagaininrevolutiontheycametheygatheredtheyworshipedtheylivedaga
ininrevolutiontheycametheygatheredtheyworshipedtheylivedagaininrevolutionheycametheygatheredtheyworship

Sermon (Song of Ourselves)

Then there was nothing left that wasn't the song & they didn't want the song but the song kept on keeping on & I didn't want the song & I didn't want to be the song but the song kept on keeping on destroying & restoring & the song thrashed about the throats & the song clattered at the ears & the song drifted below the eyes & the song seeped from stitched mouths & the song vibrated in shins & the song metered footsteps & the song rhythmed arms & the song was love & the song could not would not save a single fucking one of us but I was song & so I kept singing of this seeping/ love all the lonelier/ when I could not die—

Dear Darkness,

We have untethered ourselves the digital detritus of this system of things

We have escaped the viruses & the festering hate festooned to emptied ideologies

We have risen once again & refashioned a world in your image—

*

Yet, my dear darkness I feel like crying; like my body is tearing me to shreds

This pain has always been manifest; has always been with me

Dear Darkness,

10:48am

& I

am crushed

How does

one keep

from reading

everything as

a dialogue

of doomsday

Dear Darkness,

& they say

flesh

is demon

& they

say flesh

is

devil

&

they say

body bares

suffocating

dread

                                        *

In the woods   they said,

First heard   in   the woods

                                        They said,

                                    *

Overheard/ mixed in with branch whisper/ with worm tunneling/ with leaf rotting/ with tiny teeth chomping/ with roots intertwined with madness/ beyond the young birches/ back deep in the back of the woods/ not yet stream but/ ancient pines looming/ owl chatter/ they gathered/

They/ had given up/ they/ gave in/ then they/ rose up/ then they/ gave it/ all up/ cutting through/ the day's feedback/ amping/ it up/ & back/ out come/ evening in/ the deep/ deep woods/ they came/ they gathered/ they worshiped/ they lived/ again in/ revolution/

Sermon (When Love Alone Won't Save You)

We have undergone radical changes, have we not. We have remade ourselves not in his image! Not in the image of some imagined Almighty. Not in the image of some petty masculine deity lording power & heaven & hell & paradise over some small helpless insignificant beings!

WE HAVE UNDERGONE some radical changes have we not. Our purpose is not to be defined by our ability to worship. Our purpose is not to be defined by our ability to conform, to wait patiently while we are being stalked. **TO WAIT PATIENTLY WHILE WE HAVE BEEN HUNTED FOR CENTURIES!**

Only the fool sits silently & awaits the slaughter.
Sheep are for slaying & we are not sheep.

WE WILL EVOLVE BEYOND OUR BODIES & BECOME PURE CONSCIOUSNESS!

The Passions of the Cult

People will call it love & kill for it.   People will fear it & kill against it.

Sermon (While I Have Not Been with You, I Have Been with You)

Here we gather & I know, I know, it has been a long time since we gathered, I have been away & some of you have lost your way, I have been away & some of you felt abandoned,

The tongue forked circling the fire then flickering off into the darkness,

Death
came
to
me

& I allowed death to use me, I openly offered myself up to death

But
I
did
not
die,

Death only wants a body

& when I did not die   I was lost somewhere between here & where we are to go next,
& when I did not die   I came to truly be,
& when I did not die   I came to see the body as the vessel that ties us to tyranny

The body to be the vessel that imprisons us, that chains us to this world & its system of things

So,   I left you & so our lovely communion began to fall apart.
So,   while I was away, Death was not satisfied & some of you answered.

The murders that we found so fatiguing, the addiction to death with all the constant updates that flooded us into despair & stupidity, the world we so willingly left behind— Some of you went searching for it, some of you invited it back into our sacred center For decades, we have hidden ourselves, for decades, we have lived in this city without a name, for decades, we have made our homes inside of trees, for decades, we have made our homes on the branches of trees, for decades, we have toiled & tortured our physical beings building a city deep deep below the soil,

& one or some of you have invited that tired, old, dirty system of things right into the heart of our secret,

Right into the heart of our survival,

But fear not—

I may not have been with you, **BUT I** am always with you,

& I have seen a clear path that will lead us	away from death & destruction
I have seen the path of eternity	We ~~my brothers & sisters~~ will walk that path together
Even if they have arrived	The end days will not be the end of us.
We will leave our bodies for those that hunt it.	We will leave our bodies for those that want it.

A Warning for Those Who Do Not Believe

                                                            & the weak,

                                                        ones will die,

                                                    in their bodies,

VI.

Flowerchild

I always wanted a life in flowers
& after so many years I realized
My life had been among flowers
& then I no longer wanted a life
Of flowers, so I drifted away from
Petal, stamen, pistil, bouquet the
Bloom would have to be flesh
Or else,

Flowerchild   *

I always wanted, that is to say, I never really wanted, or I mean to say, what is it ever that I really wanted, maybe I wanted to know what it was I wanted that is to say, flowers were always around flowers, I was always drawn to & so it began without notice & so it began without plan, & so it began to take a shape & so this shape began to become my life & so the life became days stacked upon days, months bled into years & years neatly folded into decades decades of a quiet life & slow life a life filled with books & discarded stems & snipped leaves & beer & wine & so many cups of coffee & music streaming in & out the light fluctuating shading shining, shrinking so it became what I had become, not so much a choice, not as if there was a decision, sorta by happenstance by just being around, drifting, rooting, drifting, rooting, so it came to be & so the time came for it to not be, which is how I came to be here which is how I found the one which is how I found myself living in trees which is how I found myself eventually ridiculed as a revolutionary sneered at as a cult follower this is how I came to be living beneath the soil, plotting, listening, being being be,

being being be I always wanted, that is to say, I never really wanted, or I mean to say, what is it ever that I really wanted, maybe I wanted to know what it was I wanted that is to say, flowers were always around flowers, I was always drawn to & so it began without notice & so it began without plan, & so it began to take a shape & so this shape began to become my life & so the life became days stacked upon days, months bleed into years & years neatly folded into decades decades of a quiet life & slow life a life filled with books & discarded stems & snipped leaves & beer & wine & so many cups of coffee & music streaming in & out the light fluctuating shading shining, shrinking so it became what I had become, not so much a choice, not as if there was a decision, sorta by happenstance by just being around, drifting, rooting, drifting, rooting, so it came to be & so the time came for it to not be, which is how I came be here which is how I found the one which is how I myself here living in trees which is how I myself here revolutionary found myself here a cult follower living beneath the soil, plotting, listening, being being be I never really wanted, or I mean to say, I never really wanted, or I mean to say,

*

whatisiteverthatIreallywanted what is it ever that I really wanted, whatisiteverthatIreallywanted
whatisiteverthatIreallywanted what is it ever that I really wanted, whatisiteverthatIreallywanted
whatisiteverthatIreallywanted what is it ever that I really wanted, whatisiteverthatIreallywanted
whatisiteverthatIreallywanted what is it ever that I really wanted, whatisiteverthatIreallywanted
whatisiteverthatIreallywanted what is it ever that I really wanted, whatisiteverthatIreallywanted
whatisiteverthatIreallywanted what is it ever that I really wanted, whatisiteverthatIreallywanted
whatisiteverthatIreallywanted what is it ever that I really wanted, whatisiteverthatIreallywanted
whatisiteverthatIreallywanted what is it ever that I really wanted, whatisiteverthatIreallywanted
whatisiteverthatIreallywanted what is it ever that I really wanted, whatisiteverthatIreallywanted
whatisiteverthatIreallywanted what is it ever that I really wanted, whatisiteverthatIreallywanted
whatisiteverthatIreallywanted what is it ever that I really wanted, whatisiteverthatIreallywanted
whatisiteverthatIreallywanted what is it ever that I really wanted, whatisiteverthatIreallywanted

whatisiteverthatIreallywanted what is it ever that I really wanted, whatisiteverthatIreallywanted
whatisiteverthatIreallywanted what is it ever that I really wanted, whatisiteverthatIreallywanted
whatisiteverthatIreallywanted what is it ever that I really wanted, whatisiteverthatIreallywanted
whatisiteverthatIreallywanted what is it ever that I really wanted, whatisiteverthatIreallywanted
whatisiteverthatIreallywanted what is it ever that I really wanted, whatisiteverthatIreallywanted
whatisiteverthatIreallywanted what is it ever that I really wanted, whatisiteverthatIreallywanted
whatisiteverthatIreallywanted what is it ever that I really wanted, whatisiteverthatIreallywanted
whatisiteverthatIreallywanted what is it ever that I really wanted, whatisiteverthatIreallywanted
whatisiteverthatIreallywanted what is it ever that I really wanted, whatisiteverthatIreallywanted
whatisiteverthatIreallywanted what is it ever that I really wanted, whatisiteverthatIreallywanted
whatisiteverthatIreallywanted what is it ever that I really wanted, whatisiteverthatIreallywanted
whatisiteverthatIreallywanted what is it ever that I really wanted, whatisiteverthatIreallywanted

whatisiteverthatIreallywanted what is it ever that I really wanted, whatisiteverthatIreallywanted
whatisiteverthatIreallywanted what is it ever that I really wanted, whatisiteverthatIreallywanted
whatisiteverthatIreallywanted what is it ever that I really wanted, whatisiteverthatIreallywanted
whatisiteverthatIreallywanted what is it ever that I really wanted, whatisiteverthatIreallywanted
whatisiteverthatIreallywanted what is it ever that I really wanted, whatisiteverthatIreallywanted
whatisiteverthatIreallywanted what is it ever that I really wanted, whatisiteverthatIreallywanted
whatisiteverthatIreallywanted what is it ever that I really wanted, whatisiteverthatIreallywanted
whatisiteverthatIreallywanted what is it ever that I really wanted, whatisiteverthatIreallywanted
whatisiteverthatIreallywanted what is it ever that I really wanted, whatisiteverthatIreallywanted
whatisiteverthatIreallywanted what is it ever that I really wanted, whatisiteverthatIreallywanted
whatisiteverthatIreallywanted what is it ever that I really wanted, whatisiteverthatIreallywanted
whatisiteverthatIreallywanted what is it ever that I really wanted, whatisiteverthatIreallywanted

*

~~I never really wanted, or I mean to say,~~ I always wanted, ~~that is to say,~~ I never really wanted, or I ~~mean to say,~~ ~~what is it ever that I really wanted,~~ maybe I wanted ~~to know what it was~~ I wanted that ~~is to say,~~ flowers ~~were~~ ~~always around flowers, I was always drawn to~~ & so it ~~began without notice~~ & so it began ~~without plan,~~ & so it began to take a ~~shape~~ & so this shape ~~began to become~~ my life & so the life ~~became days stacked upon days,~~ ~~months bled into years~~ & years ~~neatly folded into Decades~~ decades ~~of a quiet life~~ & ~~slow life~~ ~~a life filled with books~~ ~~& discarded stems & snipped leaves & beer & whiskey & so many cups of coffee & music streaming in~~ & ~~out the~~ ~~light fluctuating shading shining,~~ shrinking ~~so it became what I had become,~~ ~~not so much a choice,~~ ~~not as if there~~ was a decision, sorta ~~by happenstance by just being around,~~ drifting, ~~rooting,~~ drifting, ~~rooting,~~ so it ~~came to be~~ & so the time ~~came for it to not be, which is how~~ I came to be here ~~which is how~~ ~~I found~~ the one which ~~is how~~ ~~I myself~~ ~~living in trees~~ which is how I ~~found myself suddenly~~ a revolutionary ~~suddenly~~ a cult ~~follower~~ living beneath ~~the~~ ~~soil,~~ plotting, listening, ~~being being be I never really wanted,~~ or I mean to say, ~~I never really wanted,~~ or I mean to say, ~~what is it ever that~~ I really wanted, ~~what is it ever that~~ I really wanted, ~~what is it ever that~~ I really wanted, ~~what~~ ~~is it ever that I really wanted, what is it ever that I really wanted, what is it ever that I really wanted,~~

System of Things & Paradise/ The Music is Coming

Hunters & the hunted
The hunters hunted
The hunted turned hunters
System of things & paradise
System of things & paradise
The music coming in waves
Crashing & collapsing
The music coming in waves
System of things & paradise
System of things & paradise

Hunted system hunters things
The coming music & paradise
Crashing hunted things &
System hunters & music
In waves system of things
Coming paradise hunted
Hunters in waves system
Crashing things collapsing
& the crashing & the
Turned paradise & system
Music collapsing crashing
Hunters & hunted the of &——

*

Sprouting/ flowers: unwanted hunters/ hunted slithered: cemetery/ unwanted: hunters I/ hunted hunter hunting/ unwanted hunted I/ hunter flesh/ hunted unwanted/ hunter shed hunted bones/ hunter-serpents hunted: burned ashed, hunter: endless holes hunted becoming/ hunter/ unwanted/ hunted flowers/ hunters slithered/ hunting darkness/ hunting into/ hunter panorama/ hunting/ flashing hunter / carcasses/ hunted becoming/ Hunter: neither/ I nor hunted/ something hunting I/ hunting/ other I/ hunted out of I/ hunter/ earth I / hunted/ the I/ hunting/ there I/ hunted/ were I/ hunting fortress I/ hunted/ upon I/ hunter reverb/ ice to/ hunter became/ I hunter tried/ hunting when I/ hunted glacier I/ hunting upon siren I/ hunter of I/ hunting/ robin imperceptible I/ hunter alive I/ hunted ripped I/ hunter self I/ head I/ hunting mouth I/ hunter agape I/ hunting/ spilling I/ hunted/ neither I/ hunter/ nor other I/ hunting/ spilling/ I/ hunted in spite of I/ hunting/ dripping/ hunter with/ worms endless/ hunted writhing darkness/ dear hunting/ unwanted upon discarded/ hunter/ agape hunted spilling/ & hunter/ spilling I/

& hunter/ spilling I/ hunted writhing darkness/ dear hunting/ unwanted upon discarded/ hunter/ agape hunted spilling/ hunting/ spilling/ I/ hunted in spite of I/ hunting/ dripping/ hunter with/ worms endless/ hunting mouth I/ hunter agape I/ hunting/ spilling I/ hunted/ neither I/ hunter/ nor other I/ of I/ hunting/ robin imperceptible I/ hunter alive I/ hunted ripped I/ hunter self I/ head I/ hunter became/ I hunter tried/ hunting when I/ hunted glacier I/ hunting upon siren I/ hunter hunting/ there I/ hunted/ were I/hunting fortress I/ hunted/ upon I/ hunter reverb/ ice to/ something hunting I/ hunting/ other I/ hunted out of I/ hunter/ earth I/ hunted/ the I/ hunting/ flashing hunter /carcasses/ hunted becoming/ Hunter: neither/ I nor hunted/ unwanted/ hunted flowers/ hunters slithered/ hunting darkness/ hunting into/ hunter panorama/ bones/ hunter-serpents hunted: burned ashed, hunter: endless holes hunted becoming/ hunter/ hunter hunting/ unwanted hunted I/ hunter flesh/ hunted unwanted/ hunter shed hunted Sprouting/ flowers: unwanted hunters/ hunted slithered: cemetery/ unwanted: hunters I/ hunted

hunter became/ I hunter tried/ hunting when I/ hunted glacier I/ hunting upon siren I/ hunter hunting/ there I/ hunted/ were I/ hunting fortress I/ hunted/ upon I/ hunter reverb/ ice to/of I/ hunting/ robin imperceptible I/ hunter alive I/ hunted ripped I/ hunter self I/ head I/something hunting I/ hunting/ other I/ hunted out of I/ hunter/ earth I / hunted/ the I/ hunting mouth I/ hunter agape I/ hunting/ spilling I/ hunted/ neither I/ hunter/ nor other I/ hunting/ flashing hunter / carcasses/ hunted becoming/

hunter: neither/ I nor hunted/ hunting/ spilling/ I/ hunted in spite of I/hunting/ dripping/ hunter with/ worms endless/ hunted flowers/ hunters slithered/ hunting darkness/ hunting into/ hunter panorama/ hunted writhing darkness/ dear hunting/ unwanted upon discarded/ hunter/ agape hunted spilling/ hunter hunting/ unwanted hunted I/ hunter flesh/ hunted unwanted/ hunter shed hunted sprouting/ flowers: unwanted hunters/ hunted slithered: cemetery/ unwanted: hunters I/ hunted & hunter/ spilling I/ & hunter/ spilling I/ & hunter/ spilling I/ & hunter/ spilling I/ & hunter/ spilling I/

*

whatisiteverthatIreally & the hurt came & the hurt became & I & I am the hurt whatisiteverthatIwanted
whatisiteverthatIreally & the hurt came & the hurt became & I & I am the hurt whatisiteverthatIwanted
whatisiteverthatIreally & the hurt came & the hurt became & I & I am the hurt whatisiteverthatIwanted
whatisiteverthatIreally & the hurt came & the hurt became & I & I am the hurt whatisiteverthatIwanted
whatisiteverthatIreally & the hurt came & the hurt became & I & I am the hurt whatisiteverthatIwanted
whatisiteverthatIreally & the hurt came & the hurt became & I & I am the hurt whatisiteverthatIwanted
whatisiteverthatIreally & the hurt came & the hurt became & I & I am the hurt whatisiteverthatIwanted
whatisiteverthatIreally & the hurt came & the hurt became & I & I am the hurt whatisiteverthatIwanted
whatisiteverthatIreally & the hurt came & the hurt became & I & I am the hurt whatisiteverthatIwanted
whatisiteverthatIreally & the hurt came & the hurt became & I & I am the hurt whatisiteverthatIwanted
whatisiteverthatIreally & the hurt came & the hurt became & I & I am the hurt whatisiteverthatIwanted
whatisiteverthatIreally & the hurt came & the hurt became & I & I am the hurt whatisiteverthatIwanted
whatisiteverthatIreally & the hurt came & the hurt became & I & I am the hurt whatisiteverthatIwanted
whatisiteverthatIreally & the hurt came & the hurt became & I & I am the hurt whatisiteverthatIwanted
whatisiteverthatIreally & the hurt came & the hurt became & I & I am the hurt whatisiteverthatIwanted
whatisiteverthatIreally & the hurt came & the hurt became & I & I am the hurt whatisiteverthatIwanted
whatisiteverthatIreally & the hurt came & the hurt became & I & I am the hurt whatisiteverthatIwanted
whatisiteverthatIreally & the hurt came & the hurt became & I & I am the hurt whatisiteverthatIwanted
whatisiteverthatIreally & the hurt came & the hurt became & I & I am the hurt whatisiteverthatIwanted
whatisiteverthatIreally & the hurt came & the hurt became & I & I am the hurt whatisiteverthatIwanted
whatisiteverthatIreally & the hurt came & the hurt became & I & I am the hurt whatisiteverthatIwanted
whatisiteverthatIreally & the hurt came & the hurt became & I & I am the hurt whatisiteverthatIwanted
whatisiteverthatIwanted
whatisiteverthatIreally & the hurt came & the hurt became & I & I am the
hurt whatisiteverthatIwanted

& When I Burn

& when I	burn then left seep	& when I	fire about scorched flat	body laid left terror
& when I	burn then left seep	& when I	fire about scorched flat	body laid left terror
& when I	burn then left seep	& when I	fire about scorched flat	body laid left terror
& when I	burn then left seep	& when I	fire about scorched flat	body laid left terror
& when I	burn then left seep	& when I	fire about scorched flat	body laid left terror
& when I	burn then left seep	& when I	fire about scorched flat	body laid left terror

&whenIburnthenleftseep&whenIfireaboutscorchedflatbodylaidleftterror&Iburnleftseepaboutscroched&I
&whenIburnthenleftseep&whenIfireaboutscorchedflatbodylaidleftterror&Iburnleftseepaboutscroched&I
&whenIburnthenleftseep&whenIfireaboutscorchedflatbodylaidleftterror&Iburnleftseepaboutscroched&I

& when I	burn then left seep	& when I	fire about scorched flat	body laid left terror
& when I	burn then left seep	& when I	fire about scorched flat	body laid left terror
& when I	burn then left seep	& when I	fire about scorched flat	body laid left terror
& when I	burn then left seep	& when I	fire about scorched flat	body laid left terror
& when I	burn then left seep	& when I	fire about scorched flat	body laid left terror
& when I	burn then left seep	& when I	fire about scorched flat	body laid left terror

&whenIleftflatbodythenIfirescrochedaboutterror&Iburnseep&Iseepburn&IbodyflatlaidfireIburnterror&I
&whenIleftflatbodythenIfirescrochedaboutterror&Iburnseep&Iseepburn&IbodyflatlaidfireIburnterror&I
&whenIleftflatbodythenIfirescrochedaboutterror&Iburnseep&Iseepburn&IbodyflatlaidfireIburnterror&I

& when I	burn then left seep	& when I	fire about scorched flat	body laid left terror
& when I	burn then left seep	& when I	fire about scorched flat	body laid left terror
& when I	burn then left seep	& when I	fire about scorched flat	body laid left terror
& when I	burn then left seep	& when I	fire about scorched flat	body laid left terror
& when I	burn then left seep	& when I	fire about scorched flat	body laid left terror
& when I	burn then left seep	& when I	fire about scorched flat	body laid left terror

&whenIfireterrorscorchedflatbodyI&IseepburnlaidfireterrorbodyIwhenfireIwhenburnIwhenterrorI&&I&
&whenIfireterrorscorchedflatbodyI&IseepburnlaidfireterrorbodyIwhenfireIwhenburnIwhenterrorI&&I&

&whenIfireterrorscorchedflatbodyI&IseepburnlaidfireterrorbodyIwhenfireIwhenburnIwhenterrorI&&I&

& when I	burn then left seep	& when I	fire about scorched flat	body laid left terror
& when I	burn then left seep	& when I	fire about scorched flat	body laid left terror
& when I	burn then left seep	& when I	fire about scorched flat	body laid left terror
& when I	burn then left seep	& when I	fire about scorched flat	body laid left terror
& when I	burn then left seep	& when I	fire about scorched flat	body laid left terror
& when I	burn then left seep	& when I	fire about scorched flat	body laid left terror

&whenIburnthenleftseep&whenIfireaboutscorchedflatbodylaidlefterror&Iburnleftseepaboutscroched&I
&whenIleftflatbodythenIfirescrochedaboutterror&Iburnseep&Iseepburn&IbodyflatlaidfireIburnterror&I
&whenIfireterrorscorchedflatbodyI&IseepburnlaidfireterrorbodyIwhenfireIwhenburnIwhenterrorI&&I&

& when I	burn then left seep	& when I	fire about scorched flat	body laid left terror
& when I	burn then left seep	& when I	fire about scorched flat	body laid left terror
& when I	burn then left seep	& when I	fire about scorched flat	body laid left terror
& when I	burn then left seep	& when I	fire about scorched flat	body laid left terror
& when I	burn then left seep	& when I	fire about scorched flat	body laid left terror
& when I	burn then left seep	& when I	fire about scorched flat	body laid left terror

&whenIleftflatbodythenIfirescrochedaboutterror&Iburnseep&Iseepburn&IbodyflatlaidfireIburnterror&I
&whenIburnthenleftseep&whenIfireaboutscorchedflatbodylaidlefterror&Iburnleftseepaboutscroched&I
&whenIfireterrorscorchedflatbodyI&IseepburnlaidfireterrorbodyIwhenfireIwhenburnIwhenterrorI&&I&

& when I	burn then left seep	& when I	fire about scorched flat	body laid left terror
& when I	burn then left seep	& when I	fire about scorched flat	body laid left terror
& when I	burn then left seep	& when I	fire about scorched flat	body laid left terror
& when I	burn then left seep	& when I	fire about scorched flat	body laid left terror
& when I	burn then left seep	& when I	fire about scorched flat	body laid left terror
& when I	burn then left seep	& when I	fire about scorched flat	body laid left terror

&I&I&I&I&I&I&I&I&I&I&I&I&I&I&I&I&I&I&I&I&I&I&I&I&I&I&I&I&I&I&I&I&I&I&I&I&I&I&

Sermon (You Think I Have Not Noticed Your Hot Eyes Wandering) (excerpt)

You do not want to go delicate here. You have poured out your heart too often. All arises from the construct of sanity. Please do not despair. Shifting. Growing shiftless. Restless. Wavering. Giving up. Given up. Backwards. Lulled in. Lot's wife. Stirring for. The system of things. Stirring for the old ways. Given up. Many of you. Your former selves humming whispering. Doctors. Lawyers. Professors. Hustlers. Longing to leave the solitude of dirt. Longing for—

But you have come this far; you have followed me. You have heard the trees; you have made a subterranean home. You have known bliss. You have known love. You have known peace. Do not waver. Steel yourself. Leave your burdens for the body. Love me as I love you. Carry a strand of my hair as your spiritual defense. We will leave this system of things. We will evolve. We leave our bodies. Do not despair. We are the next step in evolution.

VII.

Dear Darkness,

On the precipice of error over & over failure to enter

From hour to hour all this stir from day to day

A counterfeit of ignorance seeking only light seeing only in binaries

Until almost death—

Red rivers from wrist,

Young birches luminous in half-light

Surrounded in silence occasionally broken by pitter-patter

Owl here owl there of whatever life thrummed through

& connect I to that vital root & rudiment of relation

Each secret a prayer kept static & hidden

The pure bead & the emptiness,

Simultaneously basking & burning   to ascertain the mighty multitude   to be opened

To let you dear darkness breathe   to leave prayer questioned & unhinged

To become no longer a student of the light but to graduate into a greater realm

To outlive the industry of feet & hands the panorama of nature all around

Through shadows
clouds, and
darkness rest
upon it

Dear Darkness,

I prostrate myself before you

Dear Darkness,

I will shed my body before you

Dear Darkness,

Into a new consciousness I will bring them

Dear Darkness,

I live so that we can be yours—

Afterword:

Selected excerpts from *The Book of Spiritual Yearning*

Dear Lord,

You are love and your word is love and the word is love. Yet, violence abounds. In the other room their words are violence. Their bodies are violence. So much violence has been done to them. & they now do violence to each other. Their violence comes for me too.

Yet, they are devout in their worship of you. They say son always be devout in your worship to the lord. My love for you lord is boundless. & yet I have so many questions.

Dear Lord,

My brain is on fire. I have all these thoughts. All these crazy thoughts. Perhaps my love is too tender. Perhaps it burns too brightly? Perhaps it is all-consuming! When Lord, I read about the burning bush I feel that I am the bush! Lord, when I read about the fires pounding Sodom and Gomorah, I am both fire and Sodom and Gomorah! Why do I mourn for Sodom and Gomorah? Why can I not recall Lot's wife's name? Father said, remember Lot's wife. Mother said, don't be like Lot's wife. She has become nameless yet memory.

Sodom and Gomorah. Did they not live life in love?

I am trying to understand what love is and how my love for you is sacred and their love for each other was not. Maybe there was an explicit violence to their love?

Lord, your love's violence is implicit.

I have asked the pocked-faced brother who proclaims to be of your kingdom, and he says not to ask so many questions. He said my brain is unsettled because I consume too much sugar, because I do not exercise, because I have not devoted myself to proclaiming your name to the ends of the earth.

I have asked the sour-faced brother who proclaims to be of your kingdom why the sisters do not read scriptures from the stage. Why the sisters do not sit in the secret meetings to assess sins and sorries. He said, my brain is burning with the devil's divisiveness. He said that I better not let the devil dig deep into my soul. He said, ye of little faith, why ask so many questions?

I said, I am trying to understand what love is.

He said, look to your parents as exemplars.

I said, they yell at each other and they lay hands on each other in the name of rage and they leave bruises and welts all over my body. He said, to ask Brother Blah Blah, but Brother Blah Blah hates his own race. He said to ask Sister So and So, but she not-so-secretly hates all races except her own. Go ask these fine young teens who are pillars of our congregation. Beacons of light. Their voices spill forth kingdom melodies. But I say, they speak derisively of gays and all other religions as false worship worthy of their impending death sentences. They say but only the righteous will inherit the earth. Be on guard against sympathy for those wicked ways of the world, its love is restless and without the lord's approval. Be careful the ill of men will be your downfall a world of the devil's desire. You will be alone and abandoned.

Why, I asked, would I be abandoned? Would not my fine brothers and sisters lend a hand to raise me from the abyss?

He said,

they said,

Ye of Little Faith

why ask so

many questions?

Dear Lord,

I understand the day of reckoning is fast approaching. Sometimes, at night when I fall into the darkness, I can hear their hooves. It is because of this urgency that my brain is on fire. It is because of this urgency that I am asking about love.

Dear Lord,

I will
not be
lazy

each
jump-
ing
jack

my feet
apart
hands
clash

I shout
your name
I shout
my love
for you
dear
lord

hear
me
feel
me

my
sweating love
for you

Dear Lord,

I am sorry. Our history is their/my death, and we continue to kill them. Death is on the television. Their death lays foundations to the rebel music that rejects their deaths as senseless. I am sorry. Our history has been about the death of one group or another and I am still trying to understand love.

I am trying to understand why people with my mother's skin are marked for death. I am trying to understand why people with my father's skin are making marks of death. My father says to trust in you Lord, and we will be rewarded for our love. I am trying to understand my father's silence. I am trying to still love you when you have been the architect for this death.

Dear Lord,

Please help me.

ye of little faith.

I have become faithless.

Dear Lord,

I have not spoken with you. Yet, you have remained humming in my interior. I asked for your help. I grew impatient. I gave up. I attempted to end my life. The last thing I saw was a flash of light. It was you, wasn't it, my dear Lord? Even in my darkness— you let your light shine so that I may see.

Dear Lord,

I have so many questions. My brain is burning.

Dear Lord,

I have called upon you. On my knees, broken, bruised, bleeding under the bandages.

Dear Lord,

I have survived several suicides & yet, the light no longer comes to me. I long for its embrace again.

Dear Lord,

I have so many questions.

Dear Lord,

You have deserted me.

Dear Lord,

I will build a church and congregation in your name.

I will gather the many under the name of worship.

I will take us back to the beginning and we will build Eden anew.

We will not fail you. I will not fail you.

Dear Lord, you will see me.

Oh Lord,

How splendid it all is. Do you see what I have built in your image? We have left Cesar's things to Cesar. We are no longer a part of the world and that tired old system of things. Do you see how freely we now love since we have left the devil's burden to Cesar? Do you see how we have side-stepped the violence of prejudice, racism, sexism? No more murder. No more rape. No more of that failed system of things and its chains. We have left the false construct and have erected a new society in your name. In this city without a name see how we worship, oh lord. Oh, how lovely it is, our little Eden in the City without a Name.

Oh Lord,

Send me.

Send me.

I will gather them.

I will bring them.

Oh Lord,

They came. They left the classrooms, they left the courtrooms, they left the corporations, they left the libraries, they left the stage, they left the corners, they left the blacktops, and they left the playing fields and here we are. On this once toxic ground, we have dug deep into the soil, deep into the earth's warmth and have built a labyrinth of tunnels and rooms. The trees whose scars rise even heavenward we have built homes on the branches. High in the sky away from any prying eyes. Deep into the earth away from any prying eyes. We worship freely.

Oh Lord,

They no longer have phones or the internet or the daily paper and they live so freely and love so loudly & yet some of them miss the old system of things. The stain of it still spreads beneath skin. Some of them are desperate to return to their old lives. They are unsatisfied with our little *Eden*. Unsatisfied in our nameless city. Even with boundless happiness, they are restless for recklessness.

If they leave, will we become compromised? Generations have been born into our nameless city. Generations never knowing the seduction and violence of the old system of things.

Oh Lord, how to deal with those that seek to leave. How to know if their lust will destroy all that ~~I~~ we have built for you?

Oh Lord,

The one
with flowers
I have wed

The one
with flowers
has wed me.

Is this
when you
left me?

Did you
grow jealous?

Did you
feel that
my singular
devotion to
you was
compromised?

Do you think
my love for
you was conflicted?

Why did
you
abandon
me
like a jealous
father leaving
to lick his
wounds in secret?

Dear Lord,

It has returned.

The burning brain.

The need to die.

Oh Lord,

The one with flowers tells me my sleep is restless and filled with violence.

I have been having visions over and over.

Each time I attempt to kill the self I am set adrift deeper into the darkness.

Dear Lord,

Hear my supplication.

See your lost sheep.

Come collect me.

Come back to me.

Dear Lord,

The visions are clearer now. My brain no longer burns.

Please come back to me. Please, before I leave you forever.

Dear Lord,

This is my last entry.

My faith is restored & forevermore.

It was never you.

You were a necessary diversion to find my path.

I know now my purpose.

I am fortified in my purpose.

I am finished with you Lord.

I have chosen the darkness.

& when I tried to die   & when I tried to die   & when I tried to die   & when I tried to die
&whenItriedtodie&whenItriedtodie&whenItriedtodie&whenItriedtodie&whenItriedtodiedie
& when I tried to die   & when I tried to die   & when I tried to die   & when I tried to die
& when I tried to die   & when I tried to die   & when I tried to die   & when I tried to die
&whenItriedtodie&whenItriedtodie&whenItriedtodie&whenItriedtodie&whenItriedtodiedie
& when I tried to die   & when I tried to die   & when I tried to die   & when I tried to die
& when I tried to die   & when I tried to die   & when I tried to die   & when I tried to die
&whenItriedtodie&whenItriedtodie&whenItriedtodie&whenItriedtodie&whenItriedtodiedie
& when I tried to die   & when I tried to die   & when I tried to die   & when I tried to die
& when I tried to die   & when I tried to die   & when I tried to die   & when I tried to die
&whenItriedtodie&whenItriedtodie&whenItriedtodie&whenItriedtodie&whenItriedtodiedie
& when I tried to die   & when I tried to die   & when I tried to die   & when I tried to die
& when I tried to die   & when I tried to die   & when I tried to die   & when I tried to die
&whenItriedtodie&whenItriedtodie&whenItriedtodie&whenItriedtodie&whenItriedtodiedie
& when I tried to die   & when I tried to die   & when I tried to die   & when I tried to die
& when I tried to die   & when I tried to die   & when I tried to die   & when I tried to die
&whenItriedtodie&whenItriedtodie&whenItriedtodie&whenItriedtodie&whenItriedtodiedie
& when I tried to die   & when I tried to die   & when I tried to die   & when I tried to die
& when I tried to die   & when I tried to die   & when I tried to die   & when I tried to die
&whenItriedtodie&whenItriedtodie&whenItriedtodie&whenItriedtodie&whenItriedtodiedie
& when I tried to die   & when I tried to die   & when I tried to die   & when I tried to die

& when I tried to die   & when I tried to die   & when I tried to die   & when I tried to die
&whenItriedtodie&whenItriedtodie&whenItriedtodie&whenItriedtodie&whenItriedtodiedie
& when I tried to die   & when I tried to die   & when I tried to die   & when I tried to die
& when I tried to die   & when I tried to die   & when I tried to die   & when I tried to die
&whenItriedtodie&whenItriedtodie&whenItriedtodie&whenItriedtodie&whenItriedtodiedie
& when I tried to die   & when I tried to die   & when I tried to die   & when I tried to die
& when I tried to die   & when I tried to die   & when I tried to die   & when I tried to die
&whenItriedtodie&whenItriedtodie&whenItriedtodie&whenItriedtodie&whenItriedtodiedie
& when I tried to die   & when I tried to die   & when I tried to die   & when I tried to die
& when I tried to die   & when I tried to die   & when I tried to die   & when I tried to die
&whenItriedtodie&whenItriedtodie&whenItriedtodie&whenItriedtodie&whenItriedtodiedie
& when I tried to die   & when I tried to die   & when I tried to die   & when I tried to die
& when I tried to die   & when I tried to die   & when I tried to die   & when I tried to die
&whenItriedtodie&whenItriedtodie&whenItriedtodie&whenItriedtodie&whenItriedtodiedie
& when I tried to die   & when I tried to die   & when I tried to die   & when I tried to die
& when I tried to die   & when I tried to die   & when I tried to die   & when I tried to die
&whenItriedtodie&whenItriedtodie&whenItriedtodie&whenItriedtodie&whenItriedtodiedie
& when I tried to die   & when I tried to die   & when I tried to die   & when I tried to die
& when I tried to die   & when I tried to die   & when I tried to die   & when I tried to die
&whenItriedtodie&whenItriedtodie&whenItriedtodie&whenItriedtodie&whenItriedtodiedie
& when I tried to die   & when I tried to die   & when I tried to die   & when I tried to die

Sources

"Dense canopy of greenheart & bullet-wood trees" is from *Hold Hands and Die!* The incredibly true story of the People's Temple and the Reverend Jim Jones by John Maguire.

"...the value of a dead body/ Was a commodity" is inspired by the essay, "They Will Speak Loudest of You After You've Gone" by Hanif Abdurraqib.

"In the grip of a political genius who is insane" and "the bizarre death-camp of history" is from *Hold Hands and Die!* The incredibly true story of the People's Temple and the Reverend Jim Jones by John Maguire.

Sermon (We Are Only Love) was written while watching *Marjoe*, directed by Sarah Kernochan and Howard Smith.

The section beginning with, "& when I tried to die, I became a wisp of a floating thing surrounded by white sheep & pigs & a pastel sky..." uses images from the following artists: Aya Takano, Takashi Murakami, and Yoshitomo Nara.

The section beginning with, "& when I tried to die, I became the sweetly candied affections that chorus your cavities of capitulations" incorporates language from Mathias Svalina loosely adopted from the following books: *I Am a Very Productive Entrepreneur, The Explosions, The Wine-Dark Sea,* and an interview with Svalina published in Haystack Stories.

The section beginning with, "& when I tried to die, I became what the sun could not color" incorporates language from Brandon Shimoda's book, *The Desert*.

"Dear Darkness, /On the precipice of error over & over failure to enter/" incorporates language from Ralph Waldo Emerson's sermon, "[Pray Without Ceasing], 1 Thessalonians 5:17."

"& when I tried to die, I became a century of ghosts seeping from the bruised neck of songbirds" was inspired by a line from Rollerskate Skinny's song, "Ribbon Fat" from *Horsedrawn Wishes*.

Acknowledgements

Thanks to the following journals that have published poems from this book: Wendy's Subway Air Talk, Boog City, Cul-de-sac of Blood, the tiny, Heavy Feather Review, Dream Pop Press, Marsh Hawk Review, Elderly and Work & Days. Variations of some of the poems first appeared in the chapbook, *(IR)Rational Animals* (Flying Guillotine Press) and as a limited broadside by Peptic Robot Press/Joseph Lappie Art.

Thanks to Farrah Field, Joseph Lappie, Dan Magers, and Angela Veronica Wong who read versions of this manuscript and provided feedback, encouragement, inspiration, motivation and joy.

With gratitude to my wife, Hitomi Yoshio and our daughter, Emma.

Thanks to my editors Lily Lalios and Janae Mancheski for their excellent edits, enthusiasm, and careful attention to this book. And thanks to Freddy La Force for building such a vibrant press for writers.

Special thanks to Jared Hohl who read a version of this manuscript and filmed the book trailer.

Thanks for Alex Cuff, Emily Brandt, Tony Mancus, Jared White and Bill Ricchini for inspiration and friendship.

Printed in the USA
CPSIA information can be obtained
at www.ICGtesting.com
LVHW081640040424
776438LV00007B/966